Bullying in our Schools
understanding and tackling bullying
A GUIDE FOR SCHOOLS

GW00701939

About the author

David Fitzgerald is an experienced teacher, who regularly contributes to the Irish Times' 'Education and Living' section.

Bullying in Our Schools

understanding and tackling bullying

A GUIDE FOR SCHOOLS

David Fitzgerald

BLACKHALL
Publishing

BLACKHALL PUBLISHING
26 Eustace Street
Dublin 2
Ireland

e-mail: blackhall@tinet.ie

ISBN: 1 901657 73 6

A catalogue record for this book is available
from the British Library.

Printed in Ireland by
ColourBooks Ltd

Table of Contents

This Book

Nowadays, more and more questions have to be asked about the nature of bullying and what type of action could be suitable in preventing or countering it. This book is an attempt to answer some of these questions.

As a teacher and a parent, I have come across:

+ many types of bullying situations;

+ bullying situations which were handled well, and others which were handled badly;

+ bullying situations which were extremely difficult to deal with;

+ healthy, and not so healthy, attitudes towards bullying, bullies and victims;

+ lives which were devestated by bullying in the home or in the community;

+ good practice in schools for preventing and countering bullying.

I constantly meet parents and teachers looking for information on bullying and strategies for dealing with it and in this book I will share my experience with you and endeavour to support parents, teachers and school communities in keeping their communities "bully free".

Chapter 1

Understanding bullying

WHAT IS IT?

Bullying is far more than an isolated incident of aggression, which can occur between people, there is an aggressor who causes hurt or pain, and a victim, who suffers as a result and oppressive behaviour, which can continue unchecked for a long time.

Bullying causes wilful hurt which is unprovoked and repeated. The aggressor enjoys what is being done to the victim.

Bullying is, in my opinion, very aptly described by Rigby as:

Cruel, abusive behaviour which is persistent and pervasive and causes suffering to individuals which is severe and sustained.[1]

The Department of Education's Guidelines on countering bullying defines bullying as "repeated aggression, verbal, psychological or physical, conducted by an individual or group against others".

Bullying is cruel behaviour which can cause physical, mental, psychological, emotional and quite often material harm to a person or group. It is premeditated, pervasive, persistent and

---

1.   Rigby, *Bullying in Schools* (1996).

cruel treatment, which is meant to hurt and harm, and is enjoyed by the bullying perpetrator. It is wilful, conscious abuse of an individual or group, which is inappropriate and unacceptable and, by its very nature, it demands that something be done about it immediately.

THE NEED FOR IMMEDIATE ACTION

It is of critical importance for adults in any community group (e.g. a family, school, local housing estate, workplace) to deal directly, deliberately and immediately with bullying incidents or suspected incidents. Bullying is wrong, and the task of bullies appears to be to make the lives of their victims unpleasant or even intolerable. Our task, as adults in a bullying situation is:

+ first of all, to protect the victim, make sure that he/she is safe and feels safe;

+ to analyse the behaviour of the bullying party(ies) and to get them, if possible, to change this behaviour;

+ to try and ensure that the incident is not repeated.

In dealing with the bullying situation whatever action is taken aims to ensure that the bullying must stop immediately and that that those who are at risk are made safe. Further the social behaviour of the bully and the victim must be analysed and amended.[2]

---

2.   Besag, *Bullies and Victims in Schools* (1989).

We do not want to make the lives of bullies unpleasant if we can avoid it. However, it is important to remember that, irrespective of the social or economic circumstances of the bullies, all of their victims are innocent and undeserving of bullying treatment.

WHAT CAN BULLYING INVOLVE ?

Bullying can be physical, verbal, psychological or emotional and may be carried out by groups or an individual.[3]

Children who are bullied can be constantly subjected to:

+ unprovoked beatings;

+ being regularly kicked or punched;

+ continuous teasing;

+ physical harrassment in the form of shoving and pushing;

+ being called hurtful names;

+ being insulted or having their family insulted;

+ being verbally abused;

+ being threatened and intimidated by known aggressors, being bullied in school and out of school in their local neighbourhood.

+ having lies and false rumours spread about them;

+ having nasty notes written about them;

---

3. INTO, *Discipline in the Primary School* (1993).

+ being isolated from groups and being left out of activities on purpose;

+ having their property damaged wilfully;

+ living in constant fear of something bad being done to them or their families;

+ being forced to hand over money or goods through fear and intimidation;

+ being made to feel bad about themselves because they are weak intellectually;

+ being teased and jeered because of their socio-economic, intellectual, mental, emotional or racial status;

These victims can suffer physically, mentally, emotionally and psychologically, and it is obvious that they need all of the protection which we can offer them.

Bullying causes stress, pain and hurt. It impairs an individual's ability to learn, to work, to play and to live at peace with themselves and others. It is intolerable for anyone to have to suffer such damaging behaviour and such cruel repeated oppression; it cannot be excused or justified.

Chapter 2

Bullying: adults must protect children

Our message about bullies, and bullying in our homes, schools and communities, has to be clear and unambigious. Bullying is a serious form of abuse against innocent individuals, which will not be tolerated and every action possible, and necessary, will be taken to stop it. It is ongoing, persistent, pervasive and cruel behaviour through which people, young and old, can be damaged and it has to be dealt with head-on.

BULLYING OF ANY TYPE IS UNDESERVED

It has been suggested that some people, because of characteristics that make them different or distinguish them from their peers, are more likely to be bullied than others. This is totally unacceptable as bullying of any type is undeserved and cannot be tolerated.

Children who are bullied suffer unfairly and undeservedly as a result of the actions of a bully and need the protection and support of the adults in their lives. There must not be any equivocation or ambivalence about bullying behaviour. It is wrong and it damages both the perpretator and the innocent victim.

Some of our children are more vulnerable and more easily hurt by bullying than others, and, as a result, we need to be even more vigilant with them to make their lives as secure and safe as possible. The vulnerable child, who is being picked on, may be baffled by what is happening and if he/she does not have our support they may believe that in some way they have brought the bullying on themselves and so feel guilty about what is happening. As parents, we can support our children by ackowledging and understanding the unfairness of bullying. Further, we cannot accept any excuse to allow our children to bully others or to be bullied themselves.

The actions of the bullying child and the sufferings of the innocent victim have to be attended to immediately and the bullying stopped in a determined and sure-footed manner. We will support children who are being bullied and help them recover from their ordeal, but the bullies themselves also need guidance to help them change their behaviour.

MYTHS ABOUT BULLYING

There are some myths among adults about bullying which often leave children vulnerable and unprotected. I have heard adults saying such things as:

"Bullying is part of growing up. It teaches them to deal with life."

"It is good for you. It toughens you up."

"Fight your own battles. Don't tell tales."

"Ignore it and it will go away. You must be doing something to bring it on yourself."

"Come on, stick up for yourself. You won't always have us around to stick up for you."

"I was bullied and it never did me any harm."

"You've got to be tough to survive in this world. You've got to take care of yourself."

"I never interfere in difficulties between children. They have to learn to sort out problems between themselves"

I have come across situations where children were subjected to severe and continuous harrassment by other children and when I brought it to the attention of the parents, particularly the parents of the 'aggressor', I was met with an inability to understand what was happening between the children. One or more of the statements/beliefs quoted above was trotted out and it was difficult to persuade them of their need to stop what was happening. These were good parents, who took good care of their children, but they had some type of mental block when it came to bullying.

We should carefully consider the following points.

✦   If we act like this, what type of messages are we giving our children?

✦   Are we leaving them to fend for themselves in the face of a bullying 'aggressor'?

✦   Are we asking children to rely on agg-
       ression, denial and cunning to defend
       themselves, or to submit to ill-treatment
       from those who are stronger than thems-
       elves?

✦   Have we as adults forgotten the pain and
       humiliation which a bully brought on us
       as a child?

✦   Have we forgotten the fear and great un-
       ease we felt when we were subjected to
       the behaviour and whims of a bully?

✦   Have we forgotten how let down we felt
       when we were not listened to by adults
       whom we trusted?

✦   Are we really refusing not to take children
       seriously and support them when they
       are in difficulties?

When we respond to children by using one of
the replies above, we are refusing to provide
protection and assistance. We are letting them
down and leaving them unprotected. We are
really saying to them:

*It is your problem and you have to work your
way out of it. Unless you come up with a
solution and either tolerate what is happening
or overcome the bully yourself, you will not
have my approval.*

Can our good relationship with our children
sometimes depend on them not having problems?

PART OF GROWING UP: FORGET IT

Bullying, in spite of what some people would like us to believe, is not part of the rough and tumble of growing up or of ordinary everyday life. It cannot play a useful part in the child's normal development and does not as is sometimes suggested "help the child to toughen up and deal with life".

Bullying behaviour is all about gaining power over others, through violence of one type or another, and taking away their rights.

The bully derives pleasure and enjoys making others feel small. Bullies enjoy breaking people down:

+ by hurting them;

+ by physically beating them ... punching, grabbing, pushing and shoving, tripping;

+ by vandalising or damaging their possessions;

+ by blackmailing or intimidating them;

+ by spreading malicious rumours or gossip about them;

+ by taunting, mocking or jeering at them;

+ by calling them cruel nicknames which causes serious personal hurt;

+ by focussing on some physical difference or mannerism which the 'victim' possesses;

+ by isolating them and making them feel that they are not wanted by their peers.

Researchers have found that bullying of any type is damaging to the psychological and physical well-being of an individual.

Bullies can create threatening atmospheres of fear and anxiety among their victims and make life a misery through their pervasive physical, psychological or verbal violence. Besag describes bullying as a "secretive behaviour"[1] which is kept secret in so far as possible from the eyes and ears of adults. Bullies know that their behaviour is unacceptable and most of their "work" is done in secret or at least away from the view of adults who would disapprove. They are usually clever and cunning, and it is generally very difficult to catch them in the act. Even bullies, who act in front of their peers in order to display their power or to win approval, want secrecy. They are often protected from adults finding out by a "conspiracy of silence"[2] which develops in the classroom or playground.

UNCONDITIONAL SUPPORT

Children have to be able to turn to adults unconditionally. They need to be able to express their feelings, their fears and their successes openly with adults.

If children cannot turn to adults without feeling shame, fear, or weakness then we fail them.

It is hardly good enough that a child believes that he/she has to overcome a bully to win an adult's approval.

---

1.   Besag, *Bullies and Victims* (1989).
2.   *Ibid.*

THE REALITY OF BEING BULLIED

Some years ago, I noticed that one of our fifth class girls appeared to be very unhappy and always seemed to be on her own in the school playground. When I asked her teacher about this she told me that the child was usually very quiet, but of late she seemed to have withdrawn into herself. She had spoken with the child and she had been told that she was worried about her Dad, who had lately lost his job. We agreed that I would approach the child in a situation away from the classroom.

As soon as I spoke to her, the child became very distressed. She insisted that there was nothing wrong with her. When I pursued the matter she told me that she couldn't tell me what was happening to her as she was afraid.

Eventually, having given her all types of assurances, she told me that she was very unhappy as one of her classmates was constantly making cutting remarks to her about her appearance and about her Dad being unemployed. She made fun of her in front of classmates and was constantly brushing up against her and bumping into her.

She told me that she had approached her parents, who were very caring and loving, but they had told her to ignore the other girl, keep away from her and it would pass. They did not seem to understand the seriousness of what was happening. As she spoke she became even more distressed and told me that there was nothing that could be done. She told me that her parents had problems between themselves and were experiencing financial difficulties as a result of which she felt it would not be fair

to approach them again. They did not realise
the seriousness of the child's situation and
she felt totally on her own.

When I asked her why she had not approached her class teacher, or myself, she said
that she had been threatened that if she did
so she would be beaten up after school, and
that the other children in the class would hate
her for being a 'tell-tale'. The bully also threatened to injure her pet dog.

I immediately carried out a thorough invest-
igation and through confidential conversations
with other children in the class, I discovered
that what I had been told was true. The other
children had observed some of the bullying but
as they had not seen the girl bullying others
before they thought that there must have been
something happening between the two girls
and they did not want to get involved. Many of
them also told me that they were afraid of the
bully and her family.

When I interviewed 'the bully', I was quite
shocked at the vehemence with which she
denied what had been told to me. She was
adamant that there had been a row between
the two girls about name-calling and she
claimed that, irrespective of what I had heard,
she had been threatened and harrassed by
ther accuser.

Eventually, as I was getting nowhere, I told
her that I intended to bring in her parents
and the parents of the girl who was allegedly
being bullied. I knew her parents, who were
very strict, and I was curious as to how she
would react. She became deathly pale and
pleaded with me not to take this action. She
then owned up and admitted that she had been
responsible. She admitted that she had picked

on the other girl because they lived close to one another and she hated her for being a "goody goody"(her words!!). Further, she was constantly being compared unfavourably to her by her parents and she wanted to get her own back. Later, the three of us worked through the situation and the bullying stopped.

Not all cases have such a straightforward solution and some children will do everything they can to avoid admitting responsibility. Bullies often play on others' sensibilities and find the vulnerable spots which allow them to hurt their victims. They gain pleasure and satisfaction through oppressing, hurting or humiliating others and they are unable to empathise with the sufferings of others. The bully needs an excuse for the unwarranted behaviour and cannot afford to identify in any way with the victim.

Chapter 3

Bullying and leadership

CAN YOU DISTINGUISH BETWEEN A STRONG PERSONALITY, A LEADER AND A BULLY ?

Some children boss others about because they think that it is a sign of leadership. Adults, who are poor role models, may have encouraged children to think that people are important when they are in a position to order others around. They may be able to force others to bow to their will but it has little to do with leadership.

Leadership is about helping those less fortunate than ourselves by showing them what to do encouraging them, directing and leading them by our own example, to achieve success in life. Bullies, on the other hand, force others to obey them and do what they do not want to do. They use or abuse people for their enjoyment and, as it suits, they hurt them or damage them with impunity. Leadership supports and helps people feel positive about themselves, while bullying diminishes people and creates negative images in their minds about themselves.

Research and studies have shown that bullying damages children, adults and even

whole communities. The seriousness of bullying, and the damage it can do, is undisputed.
Yet many adults are reluctant to deal with it,
and even try to deny the harm that it does.
They appear to believe many of the 'myths'
which exist about bullying and have an excuse
to remain inactive and avoid doing anything
about it. They are unable to distinguish between assertiveness, achieving, winning and
bullying. They often envy and admire dominant personalities. To them, bullies often
appear to be more successful in life than their
more sedentary and passive counterparts.
They admire and envy them for their seeming
popularity and the power they hold.

SOME PARENTS' PREFERENCES

Some parents prefer their child to be aggressive and outgoing rather than quiet and
easy-going.

Many parents consider dominant, aggressive, outgoing personalities to be a happier
group of people. They consider bullies to be
better able to take care of themselves and
they believe that they will be better able to
fend for themselves later on in life. They may
even project that aggressive individuals will
cause them as parents less problems later
on. Where a highly competetive approach to
academic, sporting or social success, which
by intent makes others feel inferior or cause
distress, is seen as acceptable behaviour
bullying takes place. While there appears to
be gain from this type of approach, the 'win at
all costs' mentality is, at the end of the day,
bad, and damaging for those who engage in it

as well as for those who suffer because of it. The attitude of these type of parents "breeds complacency when it comes to dealing with the bully, and neglect when it comes to caring for the victim. It is based on the assumption that those who have an aggressive personality have a right to inherit the world. Little credit is given to the contribution made by less aggressive but more thoughtful personalities to the breadth and quality of our world."[1]

Guilty Feelings

Some parents may experience guilt about a child's bullying behaviour as it may be seen as a reflection on how the child was reared by them or even reflect their own personalities. The child may remind them of their own dominant, aggressive personality or that of their partner and they may feel responsible for the child's make-up and behaviour. They may then try to make excuses for the child's behaviour in order not to have to face up to the reality that the child they love is a bully or, in other cases, the victim of a bully.

In other cases, what a parent most admires in a child may be that very 'quality' which adds to the child's vulnerability and the possibility of them being picked on by bullies. Their outspokenness, their childish naievety, their love of dancing or music, their strength and physical prowess, their excellence at something or their gentleness and timidity may attract the attention of bullies.

---

1. Train, *The Bullying Problem* (1995).

ON BULLYING OUR MESSAGE IS LOUD AND CLEAR

Being a bully or being bullied can have devastating effects on the lives of our children if what is happening is allowed go unchecked. If action is not taken children can be given the message that bullying is an acceptable form of behaviour.

+ Bullying is never deserved.

+ Bullying is a serious form of abuse.

+ Bullies are responsible for their behaviour.

+ Bullies often try to frighten their victims into not telling.

+ If you are being bullied and you tell us we will listen.

+ We will act on what you tell us.

+ Bullying will not be tolerated and allowed to continue.

+ You have no reason to feel guilty.

+ Bullying has no positive part to play in a child's development.

+ Bullying must be brought out into the open.

+ Bullying can lead to others being bullied if you keep it a secret.

+ Bullying can lead to problems, often serious, for the bully and the victim in later life.

+ Bullying is not something to be admired.

It is good to be helpful, kind and considerate to others. If you are stronger than others use your energy to help others, not to dominate them.

WHEN PYHSICAL VIOLENCE IS INFLICTED ON CHILDREN, THEY ARE LIKELY TO DO THE SAME TO OTHERS

Bullying is totally unacceptable behaviour and something to which us adults, particularly parents, must pay great attention. It is cowardly behaviour, is unprovoked and undeserved by those who have to suffer it. Bullying differs from the ordinary rough and tumble of everyday play and the child's normal process of development.

A BULLY-FREE ENVIRONMENT BEGINS WITH ME

Bullying behaviour causes pain, hurt and suffering which may have damaging effects throughout a person's life. Children ought always to be in a position to turn to adults unconditionally for help when they experience unprovoked, undeserved and cruel treatment at the hands of others.

Inaction by adults in the face of bullying is inexcusable. Whatever fears we may have, or whatever 'evils' we think may arise from our involvement and our actions to stop bullying, they cannot be worse than the 'evils' which

befall children who are left unprotected against the cruel and callous treatment, which
a bully may dole out.

An effective slogan to adopt and act on is:

"A bully free environment starts with me."

Chapter 4

Bullying in our schools?

DO WE KNOW MUCH ABOUT BULLYING IN OUR SCHOOLS?

Bullying has always been in our schools, and in other areas in the community. However, it did not become a public issue or an issue in UK or Irish schools until the mid to late-1980s. There was a fairly relaxed attitude towards it upto then. People generally tried to avoid having to deal with it if they could as it was considered to be part of living and growing up.

However, research has since clearly shown that:

+ a sizeable number of pupils suffer at the hands of bullies;

+ it causes both short and long-term damage;

+ school and community intervention to prevent or stop bullying does help.

SOME GENERAL FINDINGS

Scandinavia

It was commonly known that there was quite an amount of bullying in schools but little research had been carried out into the incidence or consequences until the Scandinavians led the way.

Research has been carried out in Norway and Sweden since the 1970s. The two prominent figures were Heinneman in the 1970s and, later, Dan Olweus, first working in Sweden and then in Norway. Olweus did much work right through the 1970s and 1980s and up to the present day. An English version of *Aggression in the Schools: Bullies and Whipping Boys* was published (in 1978) and, among many other studies, he produced a very full study of bullying in 1993 in *Bullying at School: What we know and what we can do.*

In general, the researchers found out much of what they learned about bullying in two ways:

✦   studies asking teachers their views on the nature and incidence of bullying problems in schools.

✦   studies of children who are bullied, or are bullies, taking into account their general profiles, social backgrounds, attitudes and family influences.

A huge intervention campaign was undertaken in Norway during 1983-1985, the results of which began to come through in the late-1980s.

Some of the more general conclusions, which have been drawn from this, and subsequent research elsewhere, include:

✦   Bullying by girls tends to be more indirect than boys.

✦   Bullying is evenly divided betweeen one to one and that involving a larger group.

✦ The playground is the most likely place *for bullying in schools, but bullying can occur in classrooms, corridors and other locations.*[1]

About one half of pupils who admit to having been bullied and did not tell anyone about it.[2] This is very worrying and points to the fact that, unfortunately, many victims are either too scared or frightened to tell, are threatened so they do not tell, do not have the confidence to tell, or blame themselves for what has happened.

There is a marked difference between teachers perceptions of the incidence of bullying and actual bullying. This is due in the main to the hidden nature of some bullying and under-reporting.

Olweus[3] showed that boys, who were victims at school between the ages of 13 and 16, were, at 23, more likely to show depressive tendencies and suffer from low self-esteem.

Research into the effects of stress, which bullying causes, indicate that stressed, worried or upset pupils do not learn well, find it hard to concentrate or solve problems effectively.[4]

Bullying happens in nearly all schools and the consequences for the victim (and indeed

---

1. Rigby, *Bullying in Schools* (1997).

2. Rigby & Slee, *Manual for Peer Relations Questionnaire* (P&Q) p. 18.

3. Olweus, *Bullying at School: What we know and what we can do* (1993).

4. Turkel & Eth, "Psycho-pathological Response to Stress" in Arnold, *Childhood Stress* (1990).

the bully) can have long-term detrimental effects if support is not given.

Schools, which intervened to counter bullying, did succeed in reducing the incidence of bullying. Schools can do a considerable amount to reduce bullying.[5]

Since the 1980s, much research has been carried out in many countries including southern Australia, the UK and Ireland.

Australia

In southern Australia in the author's manual to *Peer Relations Questionnaire,*[6] the results of over 8,500 student questionnaires, from a wide variety of schools all over Australia, are described. An estimated 20 per cent of males and 18 per cent of females in the 8 to 17 age range, indicated that they were bullied weekly. Within these figures, the figure increased markedly when students entered secondary school. This certainly points to the need for work at the transition stage. The figures dropped at senior level in secondary school.

Statistics provided through KHL (Kids Help Line) in Australia suggested that the 10 to 14 age group has the most severe problems of bullying.

United Kingdom

In 1989 three important books appeared on the topic in the UK. They were:

✦   Tattum & Lane, *Bullying in Schools.*

---

5. Olweus, *op. cit.* and Roland & Munthe, *Bullying: An International Perspective* (1989).

6. Rigby & Slee, *op. cit.* (1995).

✦ Roland & Munthe, *Bullying, an International Perspective.*

✦ Besag, *Bullies and Victims in Schools.*

An excellent review on the research on bullying up to mid-1992 was carried out by Farrington in *Understanding Preventing Bullying.*

The Scottish Council for Research in Education produced two packs for circulation in schools *Action Against Bullying* (1992) and *Supporting Schools Against Bullying* (1993).

In 1990 the first large scale survey was carried out on 24 schools in Sheffield, known as the DFE Sheffield Anti-bullying Project. Its objective was to find out how pervasive bullying was and the typical age and gender differences within the phenomenon. The results confirmed the following.

✦ **Bullying was extensive in schools.**

Some 27 per cent of primary pupils reported being bullied 'sometimes' or more frequently and this included 10 per cent being bullied 'weekly' or more frequently. For secondary schools the figures were 10 per cent and 4 per cent respectively.

Twelve per cent admitted to bullying in primary schools and 4 per cent in secondary schools.

✦ **Boys were found to bully more than girls.**

The majority of incidents occurred in the playground. It was also shown amongst a host of interesting findings that school intervention had a positive impact on reducing bullying.

In Michelle Elliott's study of 4,000 5 to 16

year olds, which is included in *Bullying: a Practical Guide for Coping in Schools* (1991), she found that:

✦ 8 per cent of boys and 4 per cent of girls were severely bullied;

✦ most bullies were one to two years older than their victims;

✦ the most common advice to children from parents was to fight back. Parents preferred children to sort it out for themselves.

Ireland

In 1993/1994 Mona O'Moore, from the Trinity College Anti-bullying Unit, carried out a survey of bullying in primary and second level schools. The results to many people's surprise showed that 32 per cent of primary and 16 per cent of second level pupils had been bullied at some time. This survey is well worth reading and studying.

Guidelines for countering bullying were published by the Deparment of Education and Science in 1993 and all schools are requested to develop a policy on countering bullying behaviour.

The 'Stay Safe Programme' (a child abuse prevention programme) was also introduced into schools in the early-1990s and the issue of bullying is handled very effectively. This programme adopts a three-way approach to preventing or tackling bullying, and involves schools, parents and pupils.

OTHER MATERIALS

There is much work presently being done and there are agencies, which offer a variety of leaflets, information sheets, videos, programmes, facilitators, seminars and even library facilities. Most bookshops stock literature (fact and fiction) on the subject.

Awareness of the prevalence of bullying, the damage it causes and the need for information and support from the community to counter it, has led to a much more vigorous approach towards reducing bullying and, where necessary, tackling it.

Chapter 5

How do you know if a child is a bully?

ONCE-OFFS ARE NORMALLY NOT BULLYING

In the normal life of children rows will break out, there will be the odd fight, names will be called, lies may be told about a peer or sibling, a child may damage another child's toy in anger, threats may be made or children may exclude another child from play. When children are corrected they generally agree to stop what is happening and relationships return more or less to normal. If, however, these type of incidents are repeated on a number of occasions and you are worried about what is happening, and you think that your child may be the bullying party, it is in a child's interest to investigate thoroughly and take whatever action is necessary.

INDICATORS TO WATCH OUT FOR

If you suspect, or are told, that a child is involved in bullying, what are the signs that you should look out for? What are the indicators that a child might be involved in bullying?

✦ Their attitude and behaviour towards the parents and other members of the family is generally, or has become, aggressive. They are sullen, secretive and difficult to approach.

✦ You have received a number of reports from school, or parents of other children, about fighting or bullying. Remember that schools or parents do not relish the prospect of having to inform you that your child is a bully.

✦ A child regularly has pens, sports gear, jewellery, clothes or money which cannot be accounted for and he/she cannot account for them.

✦ You have seen a particular child deliberately hurt another child.

✦ You have evidence that a child has vandalised or damaged someone else's possessions.

✦ A child constantly tells lies about his or her behaviour.

✦ When questioned about inappropriate behaviour, your child justifies it in the most strident and often surly terms and refuses to admit to doing anything wrong, or accepting any blame.

✦ Even when the wrongdoing is admitted, there is no sense of real remorse or no sense of empathy with the victim.

✦ A child appears to enjoy hurting others and seeing them suffer.

✦ A child tells stories or makes remarks about others in order to get them into trouble. Subsequently you find out that they are untrue and even malicious.

+ Other children, even within the class-room, are nervous or silent in the particular child's presence.

+ He or she has changed friends and of late the behaviour is more aggressive and, at times, openly defiant.

+ You discover that other children tell lies to protect a particular child.

If any, or all, of these things, or a mixture of them are happening constantly, and you see patterns of behaviour emerging you need to face up to the the possibility that a particular child may be a bully and may be engaged in bullying behaviour.

DON'T IGNORE IT

You may be worried and ashamed that a child could be involved in causing harm and inflicting pain and suffering, but choosing to ignore it will not make it go away. The reality is that if a child is bullying he or she is deliberately trying to hurt others and cause them pain and humiliation. Further it is very likely that he or she is gaining pleasure from doing so. It is premeditated, pervasive, persistent and cruel treatment which is meant to hurt and harm innocent victims who must be protected. The bullying child's behaviour has to change if he/she is to develop as a healthy emotional and social member of society.

In your child's interest it is important that you do not deny what is happening and that you take the necessary action to change the situation.

TYPES OF BULLYING

Bullying can take many forms.

+   **Physical:** beating, punching, grabbing, shoving and pushing, shoving and even injuring another child.

+   **Verbal:** cruel name-calling, verbal abuse, threatening with violence, jeering, mocking, taunting, insulting, spreading gossip or rumour or telling malicious lies.

+   **Psychological:** secretly damaging or vandalising another's possessions, threatening, telling untrue stories to another to create anxieties and fears, writing graffiti in public places to make someone an object of fun or shame, writing unsigned threatening or frightening notes or letters.

Much bullying is done in secret, by whispered threats, by threatening gestures, or by physical acts which are hidden from adults. Bullies can be devious clever and cunning, and are very capable of hiding their behaviour from adults who would be in a position to take action against them.

DENIAL IS HARMFUL

Over the years, I have come across all of these different types of bullying. I have investigated incidents, spent long periods of time breaking down denial by children, supported them in admitting and then helping them change their behaviour. In the majority of cases, we have been able to stop the bullying.

However, the worst scenario for me as a teacher has been where parents, after I had checked out incidents thoroughly, denied and refused to accept that their child was responsible. They tried to excuse their child's behaviour and generally tried to pin the blame on the child who was bullied, saying that he or she had provoked their child. They refused to face up to the fact that their child could be a bully and in some cases, expressed satisfaction and pride in the fact that he/she had been able to take care of themselves.

Very often it transpired that the parents had been bullied themselves and had not received any protection from adults and, as a result, accepted that it was best if children "fought their own battles". They believed mistakenly that aggression was the way to get what you wanted.

What they said and their reactions indicated to me in that they admired and envied dominant personalities and preferred their children to be aggressive and dominant. The view of life, of parents such as have, will be mirrored by children in their attitudes and behaviours and will have a detrimental effect on their lives. In reality, children are being told that aggression, inflicting fear and pain and intimidating others, is an acceptable way of relating to others.

PROBLEMS ENCOUNTERED

Research has shown that bullies, if their behaviour is allowed to go unchecked, experience many emotional and social problems particularly later in life.

+ They cannot relate to the sufferings of their victims and have little if any sense of empathy with them. They perceive the 'bullying' as normal, even though they know that we the adults consider it to be wrong and unacceptable. They have the greatest difficulty in taking responsibility for their behaviour and they will not do so if they can avoid it.

+ They find it difficult to have positive attitudes towards others and envy them their successes. They are deprived of one of the great joys of life which is the ability to celebrate one's own and other people's successes.

+ They consider thay the victim is always to blame. When they do not get their own way they blame others. Their reasoning and emotional response are faulty. They have a lot of anger in their lives, as they find it very difficult to accept defeat in any area and they feel bad about themselves. They personalise things to an extraordinary degree. This creates a constant source of conflict with others.

+ They feel unduly threatened by everything around them. Again, they personalise and cannot seperate situations from themselves and their own lives.

✦ They may have difficulty in forming, and maintaining, healthy relationships, particularly with the opposite sex. They are more likely to get involved in difficult and often aggressive or violent relationships.

✦ Research has shown that bullies are more likely to get involved in crime later on in life.

Train (in *The Bullying Problem*) points out that two of the main characteristics of bullies are:

(a) their need and desire for power and dominance of others which distorts relationships;

(b) their feeling of alienation from the world (both the openly, competitive aggressive bully and the cunning, secretive bully) and their resentment and feeling of hostility towards others.

Train also points to the adoption of obsessive behaviour and the developing of a sense of 'paranoia' among individuals who engage in bullying over a long period.

BULLIES LOSE OUT ON LIFE

The person who bullies loses out, both as a child and as an adult. They lack the capacity to behave in an appropriate manner in their communities. They lack the capacity to reach out and seek help or receive it at times in their lives when they may be experiencing emotional, social or other personal difficulties. If people are angry with others, they will not have the trust, openess or ability to relate to others, or to discuss their feelings, that is

necessary if we are to live comfortably as accepted members of society.

TAKE ACTION

Irrespective of what questions arise, or whatever reasons are given for the bullying, it is
important that you do not deny what is happening and that you take the necessary action to
change the situation.

You, the parent, are the expert on your own
child, and most of the help and support can be
given by you. However, if you consider that
you need extra help and support it is advisable
to approach your school, or your school medical
team, and be guided by them.

The bullying situation has to be tackled and
the child supported in admitting the bullying
and accepting responsibility for the behaviour.
This should be done in a decisive, but private,
manner. We want to avoid public humiliation
of the child. We want to stop the bullying and
when the behaviour changes we want to re-
affirm the child's worth in as many ways as
possible and, when the situation has been
dealt with, we move on.

NO EXCUSES ACCEPTABLE

There is no excuse for bullying and we must
not accept any. Bullying is all about causing
hurt to others. It is generally not a one-off
occurence, but it is repeated cruel treatment
and has ongoing, damaging effects on the
victim. The bully has a reason in his/her own

mind for what is happening and gains satisfaction from treating others badly. The bully will feel a sense of power through dominating others and not have the normal sense of empathy with a person who is suffering.

Chapter 6

Why do children and young people bully?

The reasons for children bullying can be many and varied and children of any age can be involved.

The pre-school child, who has been landed in an unknown group away from the security of the mother may take out his feelings of frustration on peers.

The 12 year old who finds the transition to second level too much for him or her can be filled with fear, apprehension and anxiety of failing. The child may decide to fail on his or her own terms, and engage in anti-social behaviour, such as bullying.

Children model the behaviour seen in the home, either observing violence or being subjected to it. When physical punishment is inflicted on children they are likely to do the same to children with whom they come in contact.

The poor relationship which some children have with their parent(s), can be reflected in the negative attitude which the child has towards other children and adults. Where a parent appears to reject the child and is negative towards him/her the child may, as a result, bully other children as he/she has developed a faulty response mechanism towards others.

Some children have a low sense of their

own value and worth. They feel they are fail-
ures and are angry with the world and act
aggressively to gain attention, to feel power
over others.

Some children are victims of bullies themselves at school or at play in their locality.
They feel powerless and frustrated about the
situation and, as a result of these bad feelings,
they begin to bully others who are weaker than
they are.

They bully to gain acceptance with their
peers. In some gang situations, for both boys
and girls, it is necessary 'to prove yourself' in
order to be part of the gang.

Bullies can be jealous of other children, who
appear to be more successful than they are,
have more possessions or are more popular.
Jealousy has been found to be one of the main
reasons given by children for bullying, particularly those who have a low sense of self-
worth. They feel that life has given them a
bad deal.

Bullies lose out socially because they cannot
enjoy others successes. They often become
angry and resentful of others.

The behaviour of younger children can det-
eriorate if there is a new arrival in the family.
They feel angry as their mother or father spend
less time with them and give them less
attention. They take it out on others in the
family or, as sometimes happens, on the new
arrival.

They know that they are physically strong
and get a feeling of power from 'bossing' others
around. Again they are probably copying behaviour they experience or observe in the home
and/or in the community. They may even get
some misguided, admiring approval from certain adults for their aggressive 'macho'

behaviour.

Bullies may have some physical disability of which they are conscious but with which they have not come to terms. They feel different to other children and may even be jeered and taunted about their disability. They bully out of frustration and to feel power over others.

Because of a change in their family situation, the child may be under severe stress. The child feels alienated from the community and the bullying is a form of revenge. This change in behaviour is usually temporary and may be caused by:

✦   a parent's loss of employment and status perceived by the child;

✦   loss of the family home;

✦   a change of home and the loss of much that is familiar to the child;

✦   a death in the family or the death of a friend;

✦   the loss or death of a pet;

✦   alcoholism in the family;

✦   marriage breakdown;

✦   violence in the home;

✦   a parent or sibling in prison;

✦   poverty.

They are so insecure within themselves that they enjoy making others feel small and inflicting pain on them.

They are not used to taking turns, sharing, being part of a group, losing at any type of game or taking directions as to behaviour. They simply bully their way into getting what they want.

A child may be emotionally or mentally disturbed and as a consequence be unable to interact socially in an appropriate manner. This type of child may need medical and psychological assessment and then will need further support or treatment. The earlier the intervention is made the better, so that action can be taken to modify the behaviour.

Your child may have joined up with new friends who have a reputation for being difficult, and you might have heard that they have a reputation for causing trouble. Your child, to gain acceptance and win approval, may take on the behavioural characteristics of the gang. Is your child easily-led? They may be weak academically and are failing at school, and, as a consequence, they may feel bad about themselves, and could be inwardly angry and may be attempting to gain attention through aggression towards others.

Children may be victims of the ambivalence in attitudes among some adults about bullying. Some adults express pride and admiration when they see their child dominating other children in play. Some people have the mistaken belief that there are certain behavioural characteristics, such as bullying, which really do not harm people and are part of the normal process of growing up. Such misguided and ill-informed views encourage children to be aggressive - children absorb far more of their parents and other adults' values than they sometimes care to imagine.

Adults need to examine carefully their personal attitudes to bullying, if they are to be in a position to help children change their behaviour.

Chapter 7

Why are some children more likely to be bullied than others

FACTORS THAT MAY BE INVOLVED

Any pupil can be bullied, but some children are more at risk and prone to being bullied than others. Unfortunately, there are factors which may be used by the bully, and which may contribute to a child being more likely to be the innocent victim of a bully.

These factors can include the following.

+ Being different in any obvious way to the general body of pupils in a class or school, e.g. having a physical disability, an unusual tone of voice, belonging to an ethnic or racial group, or even being timid.

+ Lacking confidence and not being able to mix. This may result in name-calling or physical abuse.

+ Being very clever. Other pupil's jealousy can result in them being called names like 'swot' or 'lick' and I have even heard of a child being upset because he was called 'teacher'. The child's possessions and work can also be damaged and vandalised by jealous peers.

+ Being very weak academically or having special educational needs. Children who are withdrawn for remedial work are often jeered. Name calling can occur and such names as 'thick', 'spa', 'dummy', 'header' and 'donkey' have caused upset to children and in some instances led to retaliation or severe distress.

+ Children from homes where there are problems can be vulnerable and taunted or jeered. A family member in jail, a parent who is a known alchoholic or drug-user, a relative with an obvious mental problem who sometimes acts in a bizarre manner in public.

+ An overprotective parent can focus unwarranted attention on their child and hurtful jeering and name calling can result e.g. Mammy's boy or girl, Mammy's pet, 'softie' , 'sugar-puff' .

While we want to protect our children, we have to be careful that we do not draw unwanted attention to them. Teenagers are particularly sensitive about how adults relate to them in public. If your child asks you not to do something or say something in public think about it carefully. What is normal for adults may have a different meaning for the young person.

Children whose Hobbies are Different

Being a new boy or girl in the class or neighbourhood can cause a child to be bullied. This can be the result of another child being jealous of the attention, which the 'new pupil' is receiving, or because they are afraid that they will lose a friend to the new arrival.

Some children are bullied because of their hobbies, interests or pastimes. In one case with which I was involved, a boy who played hockey was mercilessly teased and taunted. The school which he attended did not have a tradition of boys playing hockey and the other boys considered it to be 'soft', a cissy's game and definitely not 'cool'. The boy in question was particularly talented at hockey and en-joyed the game. He had also been a talented football player but had not the time for both games. He was jeered about being afraid and soft.

The problem only came to light when he suddenly gave up hockey and refused to discuss why he had done so. The parents made some quiet enquiries and got to the bottom of the story. Working with the school, which took a sensitive but firm line, the issue was resolved and the boy returned to his hockey.

Children who have hobbies, which are not in line with the majority culture in a school, can become the objects of unwanted attention. They may be unjustly and without cause considered to be trying to make themselves different or to be 'snobbish'. The irony is that the very strength, talent or quality, which parents admire and promote in our children, may be the ones which cause them to be unfairly picked on.

Children's Physical Appearance

Having particular mannerisms, spontaneous physical facial movements or jerks, having prominent physical features (teeth, eyes, ears, nose, lips), wearing 'old-fashioned' clothing, being awkward or clumsy or being too small or too tall - any of these factors can lead to a child being bullied or picked on. At the teenage stage, in particular, young people are very sensitive about their appearance and their growth patterns. Personal remarks may provoke heightened reactions and if individuals or groups become aware of this heightened sensitivity they may play on it and it can result in bullying.

Children who are overweight can suffer terribly through name-calling, not being able to participate in some physical activities and being jeered as a consequence. They need plenty of support to recognise their worth and learn to accept themselves and not react to the taunting. They need to be helped to see such behaviour for what it really is - pathetic.

Sexual Undertones

Boys who do not participate in physical activities or team sports can be jeered about their sexual orientation and even considered to be reserved or 'snobbish'. Boys who are gentle are often considered by some of their peers to be effeminate or homosexual.

Many disparaging words dealing with sex and sexual orientation, which are used to hurt both boys and girls, have crept into pupil's language. Words such as 'queen', 'fairy', 'slag', 'slut', 'fag', 'bender' are used openly and need to be discussed in families and in schools.

Young people can be jeered because of their perceived lack of sexual experience and may feel pressure to become involved in, or brag about, supposed sexual activities merely to be part of the group.

Children who React Easily

The young person who becomes visibly upset and is very quick to react to jeering or name-calling may become the focus of attention of an individual bully or a group. He/she will be seen as a soft target and be seen as someone who 'is easy to wind up' and get going. Adults need to do everything possible to stop the bullies but the victim who is being so cruelly treated may also need special, or specialist, help. They will need to develop better responding skills, to boost their own self-esteem and to remain calm in stressful situations. While nobody has any right to bully them, these victims can make it easier for themselves if they know how to behave in a manner which does not attract the attention of a bully. While we cannot accept bullying it is advantageous to know how to leave a bullying situation or to avoid bringing the unwanted attention of bullies on to us.

Even Wearing Glasses!!

Having to wear glasses can cause major problems for some children and young people. Younger pupils have been known to break, hide or to purposely mislay their glasses rather than wear them. They do not want to wear them because of name-calling and jeering. Traditionally, glasses were associated with very studious people, with older people and with seriousness and dullness. Some comics and magazines still portray this image. It is advisable, if your child has to wear glasses, to talk to them beforehand - even the choice of

frames can make a difference. There are fash-
ionable frames available which may make the
whole situation easier.

Schools and families working together can
achieve a great deal in terms of developing
effective stategies to combat bullying.

Children will suffer, be hurt, or even damaged because bullying is systematic and cruel
behaviour. It is helpful to think of a family or a
school as a community where everyone has
equal rights, enjoys safety, feels free and lives
and works in a helpful environment. Within
this community, when bullies step over the
line of normal behaviour, they are guilty of
abuse and the community should take appropriate action.

Chapter 8

Developing a school policy on bullying: issues that need to be considered

A school needs a policy which promotes such values as respect, caring, tolerance and responsibility for others.[1]

ISSUES TO KEEP IN MIND WHEN DEVELOPING A SCHOOL POLICY ON BULLYING

For a school policy on bullying to be successful, and before we can implement effective strategies to prevent or combat bullying, a number of factors have to be taken into account.

1. Involve All Groups

When we are considering bullying in the school context, all members of the school community need to be involved in the development of a policy and their support canvassed. Teaching and non-teaching staff, parents, pupils, parents' groups and the board of management.

---

1. Byrne, *Coping with Bullying in Schools* (1993).

2. All Understand and Agree

It is a school community problem to raise awareness and take action against bullying incidents and everyone has to be committed to the school policy

The policy needs to be understood and accepted by all and be supported by structures within the school that ensure its implementation.

3. Raise Awareness

An integral part of the policy is to raise awareness of bullying: where/how/when it happens, the symptoms, the damage it does to both the bully and the victim.

4. Myths

Some of the myths around bullying have to be removed:

+   big boys and girls don't tell tales;

+   everyone is bullied at some time and it is part of life;

+   bullying toughens you up and prepares you for life;

+   it is a sign of weakness to ask for help and you should be able to fight your own battles.

As bullying is so difficult to deal with, adults often prefer to ignore it or avoid it and hope that it will go away and not reoccur. It is worthwhile asking ourselves as adults if we would tolerate bullying in our own lives. I am certain that we would not, so why should we expect children to accept and put up with it?

5. No Ambivalence: Protect the Innocent

The policy is there to:

+ state clearly and unequivocally that bullying is totally unacceptable in the school commmunity. The bully is at fault and has to be dealt with and the policy will protect present and potential innocent victims;

+ recognise that most bullying takes place in secret, can be very difficult to detect, is highly likely not to be reported and, when detected or reported, needs be dealt with firmly and decisively;

+ ensure that action is taken to stop bullying immediately it surfaces and effective action is taken against those who engage in it. There need to be clear guidelines;

+ try to change the behaviour of the bully and allow him/her to make a fresh start;

+ help the community to differentiate between 'normal aggression' and bullying;

+ prevent bullies hiding within a group over which they have power;

+ develop effective strategies which will prevent bullying occurring or reoccurring.

6. Rehabilitation

The objective of dealing with the bully is to obtain repentance and an assurance that the behaviour will not be repeated: we want to rehabilitate, not annihilate, the bully.

7. Strategies to Avoid Bullies and Bullying

While victims are in no way responsible for being bullied, it is advisable to teach them how to avoid bullies and bullying situations, for example:

+ how to react to name-calling or teasing;

+ not to bother responding to particular people;

+ how to be calmly assertive and avoid anger which often gives the bully an excuse.

8. Open Atmosphere

The best way to prevent, or counter, bullying is to recruit everyone in the school to that purpose.

The policy deals with school procedures and expectations about bullying in the classrooms and around the school, and will aim to create an atmosphere where it will be safe for anyone to report incidences of bullying.

9. Adults

Adults have a particular responsibility to protect children from bullying or potential bullying.

10. Awareness of Bullying

Highlighting the issue of bullying will not suggest that your school is a bullying school. Bullying can occur in any community and because of the serious nature of the behaviour, it is necessary to have a high level of awareness of bullying, to know how to prevent it and what to do if it occurs. If a school has an agreed, effective code of discipline, is well organised, and works in the interests of the pupils, it will ensure that bullying is kept to a minimum. Parents will welcome this.

Bullying is a serious problem and does damage to pupils and adults who are caught up in it. It is a form of anti-social, unacceptable behaviour which cannot be tolerated.

11. A Written Policy

The school community will benefit if there is a clear, unambiguous written policy to counter bullying, which makes it clear to all in the school community that any member of the school community who is involved in bullying behaviour, will be disciplined immediately, severely and in accordance with agreed procedures.

Chapter 9

The development of the policy on bullying

THE BEGINNINGS

Form a Committee

It is advisable to form a committee to set out what has to be done before a school policy can be developed and agreed on by all. If you want to ensure that the policy works everyone in the school community has to be part of the process.

The committee can be made up of:

+ teachers, parents representatives, the board of management and representatives of pupils and ancillary staff at second level;

+ teachers, parents representatives, the ancillary staff, board of management and will need to have a structure for consulting with the representatives of the pupils and at primary level.

The main task of the committee is to develop an anti-bullying policy in consultation with all the groups in the school, building on what the school is doing well already implementing the policy and later on revising it.

Give Time for it

Time is a factor that will have to be considered as everyone in the school community has other priorities to deal with as well. Time is needed for:

✦   initial meeting(s);

✦   compiling questionnaires;

✦   administering the questionnaires. They all need to be completed on the same day to avoid discussion which may influence and colour some of the responses;

✦   gathering and analysing the information;

✦   examining and evaluating the information;

✦   meetings to look at how the questionnaires' information is to be managed and presented;

✦   meetings to work on the development of the policy and its subsequent implementation

THE WORK: WHAT HAS TO BE DONE?

To develop a school policy you can work through the following steps.

1.   Outline in a 'school statement' what you want for the school and why you need a school policy.

2.   Move on to what elements you need to include in the policy.

3.   Follow up with the development of the policy itself. Review present resources,

identify needs and identify where gaps are. At this stage you have to prioritise what has to be done.

4.   Then take action. The policy has then to be communicated and implemented.

5.   Lastly it has to be reviewed on an ongoing basis.

THE WORK OF THE COMMITTEE

1. A School Statement

The first area to consider is the development of a school statement on bullying. This statement merely states the importance attached to a bullying policy in the school This is a simple, but necessary, process, and there is no mystique about it. A statement sets out in simple terms the school's philosophy and what the school wants and intends to strive for in the future.

This statement will:

✦   be an amalgam of the perspectives of the different groups in the school as to what kind of school they want;

✦   represent the school community's hopes in terms of positive behaviour and doing everything possible to eradicate bullying.

✦   be the school's vision and what they will build towards for the future.

This statement must be clear, simple, feasible, realistic and workable and some time should be given to devise an agreed and clearly understood version. Commitment to the statement

will be vital if the school policy to raise awareness of, prevent and (where necessary) counter
bullying is to work.

A statement can be as short as the following:

*The community in St Mary's school wants to
ensure that all in the school community, particularly the pupils, can live, work and play in
an environment which is totally free from
bullying.*

This statement says a number of important
things.

✦   There is a community in the school: a
      community of adults and pupils who live,
      work and play together.

✦   That the community will co-operate and
      do everything possible to ensure that all
      pupils, irrespective of their ability, age,
      social, or economic circumstances, can
      go about their daily lives, learn, play and
      be happy together in school and be prot-
      ected from bullies and bullying.

✦   The community's effort to keep the school
      totally free from bullying will command
      its total commitment. There will be no
      equivocation or ambivalence about bully-
      ing. Bullying is out and not wanted.

When a statement of this type is agreed on,
the members of the committee give a commitment to leave no stone unturned to achieve
their ultimate objective. It will strive to develop
a happy school community in a totally bully-
free school environment. It wants to have a
school which takes care of all of its pupils and
adults and promotes goodwill between them.

The school statement will drive the policy
on which the committee can then start to work.

2. The Elements of the Policy

Once the policy statement has been agreed on, your committee will start the work on the elements to be included in a framework for a school policy and then examine the process for developing it.

Before you develop a policy, you will need to look at the following areas.

+ The role of the board of management in the development of the policy.

+ Any training needed for the different groups. Can outsiders assist?

+ How the work will be co-ordinated and/ or who will lead the project?

+ If there are extra resources needed, who will provide funding for these?

+ How are meetings to be timetabled?

+ How are the different groups to be kept informed?

+ How will it be reviewed and evaluated to see how well it is working?

+ What elements should be included in it? The framework for a policy?

+ Parental, pupil, teacher and other staff involvement.

+ Measures for raising awareness of the causes and effects of bullying: for prevention, countering bullying, ensuring support for all victims, analysing the bullying behaviour, punishing and, hopefully, rehabilitating the bully.

One of the major tasks is developing the plan and this involves:

(a)   raising awareness;

(b)   increasing understanding of bullying;

(c)   planning together.

This can be done through information and discussion meetings on the topic, looking at the findings from the questionnaires, accessing other relevant information, looking at attitudes, developing strategies, using the curriculum, looking at school ethos and examining good practice from other schools.

When it has been decided what will be included in the policy framework, and arising out of the discussion, members may have concerns about particular aspects of it and these may necessitate additional attention being given to them. For example:

✦   Who should be consulted?

✦   How will you communicate the policy with the parents?

✦   How will you communicate the policy with the local community to ensure their support for the school?

3.   The Process of Developing the Policy

Before you draw up a policy document, it is important to find out what is happening in the school and identify the needs of the school in relation to bullying.

You will need to look at a number of factors and issues relating to the school community.

1. Reviewing the Existing Policy. What to do?

Start at the beginning, and find out how much bullying is going on in your school? (Questionnaires to teachers and selected classes/ interviews for younger pupils/group discussions)[1]

• Which Pupils are involved?

What does it involve and what type of behaviour does it involve?

Is it direct (physical harrassment, teasing or taunting, name-calling, making insulting, demeaning or threatening gestures, abusing, threatening, openly taking another pupil's possessions) or indirect (having possessions damaged or stolen, anonymous notes or letters, nasty rumours about the pupil or relatives relating to sexual orientation or behaviour or social standing, being isolated and deliberately excluded by individuals or groups)?

✦ What is the most common type of bullying, and why?

✦ Which group of children are most often bullies or victims and why?

✦ Where does it happen? (Playgrounds, toilets, corridors or classrooms.)

✦ Are adults told about incidents?

✦ What do we do about them?

✦ Are pupils happy with our response?

✦ What do they think teachers should do?

✦ Are we happy with our own response?

---

1. See Appendix 4 where we have questionnaires for all groups.

+ What else might we do?

+ What are parents' views on the level of bullying and the school policy? This can be determined by sending questionnaires to a sample of parents.

+ How can pupils and parents support teachers and management in preventing and, where necessary, countering bullying?

+ What is being done at present to support an anti-bullying policy through the code of discipline, through the formal curriculum and through the culture and ethos of the school. (The hidden curriculum?) Draw up a list, at this stage without comment.

+ What is the behaviour like at present?

+ Is there bullying in the school?

+ What is the extent of it?

+ Who is involved?

+ Where does it happen most often?

+ Why is it happening?

+ What information about bullying could you gather from pupils, parents, teachers, other staff and management? This can be done most efficiently and effectively through questionnaires and interviews.

+ What is the level of awareness of the implications of bullying on victims, bullies themselves and those who have to observe it?

+ Does the atmosphere and quality of relationships in the school community support bullying?

+ Are there aspects of the curriculum in the different subject areas being used to support and reinforce it?

+ Which groups are involved at present?

+ Are there groups whose support would be valuable who are being neglected, e.g. voluntary groups, ancillary staff, sports' coaches?

+ Are there particular pupils who will require special support, e.g. children who have special needs, children from violent or aggressive families?

+ Do we recognise that there are some children who are more vulnerable to bully, or be bullied, and they require special care and attention?

+ Do some of the parents, teachers and pupils have some ambivalent thoughts and feelings about bullying?

+ Are there troublespots in the school which need particular attention to be paid to them? For example, the toilets, the playground, the stairs, walkways in the grounds or the washrooms and dressing rooms. Going to and from school on the bus causes huge problems for a number of pupils. Is anything being done about these troublespots?

+ What is the level of co-operation among parents, staff, pupils and management to keep bullying at bay? Is the atmosphere in the school conducive to encourage children/parents/ancillary staff and others to report bullying incidents?

+ What does the code of discipline (the code for promoting positive behaviour) say about bullying?

+ Would changes in the code improve the situation in the school? What new discipline procedures (punishments) and changes need to be introduced?

Structured verbal interviews should be given to the younger children and others for whom they would be more appropriate than the written questionnaires.

Getting information on, and insights into, issues associated with all the above is generally best done through a mixture of written questionnaire and verbal interviews with the different groups in the school.

Structured verbal interviews will be given to the younger children and others for whom they would be more appropriate than the written questionaires.

You can devise your own questionnaires and I have included samples which may be of assistance (see Appendix 4). They will need to be redesigned and changed in order to meet the circumstances which prevail in your school.

Benefits from Filling in the Questionnaires

When individuals fill in the questionnaires they are:

+ giving their picture of the school situation in relation to bullying;

+ raising their own awareness of bullying and its effect on pupils;

+ thinking about solutions;

✦   hopefully recognising their rights not to be bullied;

✦   starting to report, which is the key to success.

Very often after they have filled in the questionnaires there will be an increase in reported bullying in the school. Some people read this wrongly, and if they are allowed they will blame the awareness raising process for an increase in bullying. However, if reporting increases it must be recognised in itself as a sign of the success of your initiative. Pupils and/or adults are developing more confidence and feel more free to report to the relevant authorities. After this what action you take will determine whether you will have further success or not.

In working through the information gathering/finding out process our own level of awareness will be raised of what bullying is about. What is actually happening? What attitudes need to be worked on? What information teachers, parents and pupils need? What action needs to be planned for to work to raise awareness among the pupils and the parents?

It is best if there is a whole-school approach to bullying: everyone in the school community needs to plan and agree on the basis of our findings and what action is necessary. This involves the drawing up of a clear plan on what to do and how to act.

If there is an agreed plan, it will ensure a consistency of approach among adults and a clear understanding among pupils of what is acceptable, the consequences of being involved in bullying and an assurance and understanding that support will always be available.

4. *When you have Identified the Needs and Reviewed the Present Provision, you can Prioritise What Needs to Happen and Develop a Shared Plan*

5. *Then Implement the Plan and the Procedures and Take Action*

Introduce new practices and new ways of behaving that characterise day to day activities and events in the life of the school.

6. *Build in Evaluation and Review Procedures into the Plan to Check How Well it is Working*

+   Is it working?

+   Is it doing what we set out to achieve?

+   What do we need to change?

Chapter 10

What should a policy contain?

Activities for raising awareness among the whole school community and delivering the message of our school statement are considered below.

1. The Use of Programmes or Sections of Programmes

For example:

+ *The Stay-Safe Pack and Video* (Eastern Health Board).

+ *On my own Two Feet* (Deptartment of Education and Science, Marlborough St, Dublin 1).

+ *We Don't Have Bullies Here* (VE Besag 57 Manor House Road, Jesmond, Newcastle upon Tyne, NE2 2LY, UK).

+ *Action Against Bullying: A Support Pack for Schools* (Johnstone, Munn and Edwards, 1992).

+ *Supporting Schools Against Bullying* (Scottish Council for Research in Education, 1993).

✦   *Kidscape* (ISPCC and The National
     Parents' Council, post-primary 20
     Molesworth St, Dublin 2).

There are videos   (e.g 'The Stay Safe Programme' videos from the ISPCC and Barnardos)
and books (see the booklist in Appendix 8),
which deal with the subject of bullying which
can be displayed in the parents' room and/or
shown at parents' evenings in conjunction with
workshops or talks.

In some schools, the practice has grown
where students attend these evenings with
their parents, which I consider to be a very
wise and beneficial practice. Children, parents
and teachers get the same message.

Videos can also be used during class, on
open days or during a 'Bullying Awareness
Day/Week'.

A BULLYING AWARENESS WEEK

This is a superb idea, and should involve a
strong curricular base and a high level of
parental involvement.

How does it Work?

A Bullying Awareness Week can be an enjoyable and fruitful project for all in the school
community. It involves a period of time during
which there will be a planned focus on bullying. All in the school will be involved in some
activity related to bullying. Parents, pupils,
maintenance staff, the bus driver, the traffic
warden, the local community, the teachers
and the board of management.

A set period of time is allocated where, through different types of related class activities and some project work, there is almost total focus on:

+ raising awareness of bullying and learning about the detrimental effects it has on our lives;

+ creating the confidence within the school community which ensures that everyone will protect their own, and other's, rights, take action and report bullying, or suspected bullying. We want people with a high sense of self-worth who do not bully others, or allow themselves to be bullied;

+ building on and adding to the climate of trust, respect, equality, kindness, care and consideration for others in the school community.

Motto for the Week

A starting point can be to devise a motto for the week. All you need is a simple statement of what you hope to achieve or the school philosophy. For example:

In St Paul's adults and pupils (or pupils and staff) treat each other with respect. We do not bully or tolerate bullying.

In St Paul's we believe that every member of our school community has equal rights. We all work for each other to ensure that we can learn, play and live together without bullying.

Keeping St Paul's a bully-free school begins with me.

St Paul's pupils and staff work together to create a peaceful and happy school environment where everyone is safe and happy.

THE ACTIVITIES

1.   Pupils work on bullying through a combination of the following activities:

+   creative writing;

+   an art competition (pictures and posters);

+   group collage of bullying situations, streamers, banners;

+   gymnastics;

+   drama and mime;

+   storytelling: their own experiences of bullying or reading stories from literature;

+   class discussion and debate;

+   classwork on definite planned sections of programmes such as 'The Stay-Safe Programme' or 'On my own Two Feet'.

Each class has a number of planned periods dealing with sections of these or other programmes. We ensure that every child is deals with the broad aspects of bullying in class during the week. This is a key part of any bullying awareness week.

2.   Parents and other staff work together and with teaching staff on bullying through:

+   participating in creative writing or art

competitions (this has been done very successfully);

+ telling their stories of bullying to pupils, telling about incidents from their own school days;

+ reading from literature to pupils;

+ attending and supporting the pupils' drama presentations;

+ attending talks (very often information evenings or mornings) followed by discussion, which are facilitated by parents/teachers/psychologists on bullying or related topics which have been organised by the Parents' Association or the board of management. These talks/discussions can provide information on the different issues related to bullying, raise awareness of bullying, and examine the attitudes of teachers, parents and other adults towards bullying;

+ working with teachers on organising competitions for pupils or the wider community;

+ obtaining sponsorship;

+ organising displays;

+ informing the wider community of the school's efforts (ethos) and involving them;

+ seminars/discussion groups/videos/on topics relating to bullying for parents, pupils, teachers and the wider community;

It is important to examine the School Code on preventing and countering bullying the week.

Raising awareness, examining attitudes and providing information for parents, teachers and other staff will be the main focus of the work done here.

3.   Teachers work on bullying through:

+   organising creative classwork or projects on bullying;

+   organising drama from the class or an outside drama group;

+   accessing literature for pupils on bullying

+   relating stories of their own;

+   organising competitions;

+   working with parents on displays and parents' inputs;

+   organising sponsorship for the competitions.

4.   The wider community:

As the school is very much part of the wider community, it is important to involve the community in events such as The Bullying Awareness Week. They can develop further confidence in the school from attending activities during the week (e.g. the writing or art displays and the drama) and/or provide sponsorship for some of the events.

AFTER THE BULLYING AWARENESS EXERCISE

Subsequent to the bullying awareness week the school can produce a magazine outlining the events of the week. In addition to being a celebration of all of the school's activity the magazine can be used later by parents or teachers to reinforce the anti-bullying message. A copy of the school's code on bullying can be included.

Teachers, parents and pupils who are involved in this awareness raising exercise will learn a lot of new things about bullying, how it affects people and the need for agreed action when incidents take place.

WILL OUR SCHOOL BE SEEN AS HAVING A PROBLEM?

Some teachers and parents had fears that having a 'Bullying Awareness Week' might send out a message that their school had a problem with bullying but, thankfully, this has not been the case in any school where I know that the exercise has been undertaken. In fact, the focus on bullying for a week enhanced the pupils', teachers', parents' and the wider community's confidence in the school. The school sent out a strong message that they would leave no stone unturned to keep bullying out of the school.

OTHER IDEAS

1.   An incident or suggestion box in a prominent position within the school building which may be used by any of the pupils, or adults in the school community.

Have you tried using it? It can, of course, deal with all aspects of behaviour and it is certainly worthwhile giving it a try.

2.   Inputs about bullying in the curriculum during English, art, drama, civics, social and political education, religious knowledge and history classes.

3.   Creative writing in story or poetry. I have read some wonderful poetry which was written by pupils and parents. They dealt with bullying incidents, word-pictures of victims and bullies, descriptions of incidents and descriptions of feelings.

One of the most powerful pieces I read was a description of a bully and how he felt as he humiliated two smaller boys in front of his on-looking friends.

Another poem described the fears of a child, whom I taught, before she went to the play-ground and her terror as she tried to hide and almost make herself invisible. The crouch-ing figure of the terrified little girl and how she felt were very strong and left me numbed.

Other pieces described:

+   a pupil who was getting threatening telephone calls;

+   a pupil who was being called names;

+   an old man who was being harrassed by unthinking young people;

+   a bully who was harrassing old people;

+   a boy who was being picked on by a gang;

+   a girl who had been isolated by her friends.

The descriptions of the bullies, their victims and their respective feelings about themselves were very real and very informative about the children's and adult's individual perspectives on bullying.

A number of adults were given a few topics and asked to write either a poem or a story for use during part of a class or even a 'Bullying Awareness Week' (see Appendix 1). Some of the parents read out their work and this was very effective. This was a creative, challenging, awareness-raising exercise for adults and as I later found out an enjoyable and profitable exercise for the pupils.

The adults also derived enjoyment, information and new ways of looking at bullying from their own work, and also from the work of the pupils.

4. Art work on similiar topics as the writing, involving adults and pupils is a creative and enjoyable method of raising awareness and setting people thinking about bullying. You can:

+ paint;

+ use charcoal, black and white charcoal drawings or abstract pictures are very effective;

+ newspaper collage, print, photos, designs made from torn paper;

+ make papier mache or plasticine models;

+ do pencil drawings;

+ design posters with or without illustrations, warnings, short pithy sayings, statements about rights, descriptions of bullies on 'Wanted' posters or 'Reward' posters to encourage pupils to report incidents.

5. Bullying looked at from literature: poetry, novels or biography, fairy tales and fables. For example:

+ *My Parents Kept me from Children who were*

Rough (Stephen Spender) is a wonderful poem to examine with senior classes in primary or junior classes at second level, the bullying boys, the child who is definitely susceptible to bullying, the avoidance measures which he tries, their respective feelings about each other, etc.

✦   Novels and short stories.
  Tom Brown's School Days
  Oliver Twist
  David Copperfield
  A Christmas Carol
  Cinderella
  The Ugly Duckling
  Rapunzel
  Jack and the Beanstalk
  Joy Chant, *Red moon & Black Mountain*
  C S Lewis, T*he Lion or The Last Battle*
  Pat McCabe,*The Dead School*
  Jas Plunkett,*The Trusting and the Maimed*
  Rudyard Kipling, *The Jungle Book*
  Jane Austen, *Pride and Prejudice.*

Enquire at your local library and bookshop and they will advise you on what is available.

6.   Inputs during other classes. For example:
History
✦   Parts of the world where people are being bullied/discriminated against today, e.g. south eastern Europe, southern Africa, Rwanda.
✦   Slavery, the history of the cotton plantations.
✦   Discrimination over the centuries in work against women and children, e.g. the Industrial Revolution

+ Unjust laws, e.g. the penal laws, apartheid laws.
+ The history of suffrage in Ireland and Britain, e.g. Margaret Cousins, Emily Pankhurst.
+ The contributions of different people coming from different sections of society, e.g. Nelson Mandela, Martin Luther King, Mahatma Ghandi.

Civics (CSPE)
+ The rights of citizens.
+ Gender equality.
+ Bullying in the workplace; many incidents involving men and women are reported in the newspapers.
+ Racism.
+ Dealing with disability.
+ Old age: the contribution that older people make to society and the problems for them arising from the cruel treatment to which they are often subjected.

AN AGE AWARENESS WEEK

In some communities it is not unusual for old people to be taunted, teased, called names and harrassed by a minority of unthinking children and young people. To combat this in my own area we organised an 'Age Awareness Week' with local community groups. It involved:

+ A concert in the school where the pupils performed for the old folk and some of the old people sang, played music and danced for the pupils. This was followed by the children serving a meal to the old people.

+ Discussions during class about the benefits which old folk bring to the community. The great majority of pupils saw their own grandparents and older relatives as very important in their lives and valuable members of the community. They were horrified to think of anyone abusing them, and yet some of them admitted to making fun of other old people.

+ Discussions in class on how to support old people in the community: running errands, helping with gardening, visiting

+ Groups listening to older people describing their lives, showing their skills, describing what they had worked at, sports with which they had been associated, what annoyed them. There are groups of retired people (e.g.The Association of Older People) who supply speakers.

+ Pupils writing, doing some art about their grandparents or situations involving old people.

+ Drama and role-play: children of all ages love this type of work and they learn much from it. In addition, we can observe much from their work about what is happening in the school and in their lives.

When dealing with bullying themes or role-play watch out for the child who scoffs at and tries to belittle the exercise. Have they something to hide, or are they trying to intimidate? The child who is timid or appears to be repressed may also give you clues.

The exercises in themselves, while awareness heightening, are also very enjoyable and entertaining. We have produced short dramas on, for example:

+ bullying on the bus;

+ old people being bullied;

+ a classroom bullying episode;

+ the sneaky bully;

+ the new girl who was miserable;

+ a bully I hate.

Young people can be imaginative on stage. They can learn much and we can learn much from them about what is going on in their lives.

Religion

Equality, different talents, respect, love of God and love your neighbour, pride, greed and bullying: stories from texts and from *The Bible*.

Social and Personal Education (SPHE)

+ Developing self-esteem and helping pupils grow into independence in a caring school community environment.

+ Supporting each pupil in recognising:

  (a) their own self-worth and their right to voice their opinions;

  (b) the benefits of asking for, and receiving, help;

  (c) their right not to be bullied and to seek support if it arises in their lives;

(d)   their responsibility to take care of those weaker than themselves;

(e)   the importance of talking to others if they are troubled or being bullied. Breaking down the barriers, particularly for males in our society, of showing and expressing their feelings. Giving them the confidence not to have to live up to images which suggest that it is a sign of weakness to seek help or to express our fears and anxieties to others.

Peers can put tremendous pressure (which can be a type of bullying) on young people to engage in activities which they would prefer to stay away from and schools can support them in developing skills to make up their own minds and make good choices. The activities in question can vary from drug taking, smoking cigarettes, consuming alchohol, bullying another child, isolating another pupil from the gang, annoying pupils or adults who are different in some way to delivering, selling, buying or taking illicit drugs.

There is much good work being carried out in schools at present, particularly in the social, personal and health education areas and class teachers, teacher counsellors, special support teachers and guidance counsellors at second and primary level use a variety of materials.

The issues covered, all of which relate to bullying, include:

✦   What is bullying?

✦   What are the pupils' views on bullying?

✦   Is bullying acceptable in my family, or in my school?

+ What is the difference between bullying and rough play?

+ Why do people bully (adults and children)?

+ How do bullies or their victims feel?

+ Why do some people enjoy hurting others and causing violence?

+ Can bullying ever be good?

+ Can bullying help people?

+ Why do some people not tell?

+ Why is it important to tell?

+ What can I/we do to stop others bullying?

+ Feeling good about myself and others.

+ Why we share (give and receive)?

The extent to which any of these approaches is successful depends on how purposefully and meaningfully they have been used, and how relevant they have been made to the pupil's lives. The pupils must find the activities interesting if their awareness is to be raised and if they are to have the desired effect.

THE HIDDEN CURRICULUM: HOW WE COMMUNICATE WITH AND TREAT EACH OTHER?

Developing a sense of self-worth, and helping adults and pupils in the school community feel good about themselves, should permeate all communication and work within the school.

How do we speak with and how do we treat pupils? Do we treat them equally or respectfully? Do they feel equal and valued?

How we treat each other as adults (parents and teachers) will be seen, and is likely be imitated, by pupils.

How we speak to one another, the language we use, will again be modelled by the pupils and imitated and will be a big factor in determining the atmosphere in the school. In our communication do we promote equality and respect for each other?

If we are to avoid bullying or any semblance of bullying we must treat all others irrespective of age and size with equal respect. Pupils will not be respectful of others, particularly those smaller or weaker than themselves, if they are treated badly by adults, especially significant adults, such as parents and teachers, whose behaviour they are likely to copy.

The atmosphere and culture in the school has got to give the following message to pupils:

If you are being bullied in any way you've got to tell somebody. Don't accept bullying. Tell a teacher or your parents or an adult who will do something about it. In our school we will listen, help and support anyone who comes to us and we will not allow anyone to bully you.

Don't wait. Tell someone as soon as possible. You are helping the bully by not telling.

We respect pupils who stand up for their own and other's rights to live and work in a school that is free from intimidation.

Pupils can be supported in:

+ recognising bullying;

+ being informed about it;

+ seeking help;

✦ not allowing themselves to be bullied;

✦ learning how to deal with and/or avoid bullying situations.

It is likely that within the school community, or even in a neighbouring school, that there is an individual with training in teaching assertiveness techniques and supporting pupils in developing a healthy level of self-esteem, which they can use in situations where they are being bullied.

Pupils can be taught to:

✦ be assertive;

✦ make their own decisions about saying yes or no in particular situations;

✦ resist threats or intimidation;

✦ recognise and resist manipulation;

✦ respond to teasing and name-calling;

✦ ask for help and support;

✦ recognise their own worth and strengths and not be dependant on others for self-worth and affirmation;

✦ be satisfied with their best efforts.

IT IS BENEFICIAL TO HAVE SCHOOL ASSEMBLIES AND CLASSROOM DISCUSSIONS WHICH DEAL WITH THE TOPIC OF BULLYING

During the development of the plan, it is beneficial if everyone's ideas and opinions can be heard. If everyone in some way is consulted,

listened to and is part of the plan/policy
development process they will be highly likely
to buy into it and work it. Finding time for the
work is a big issue for schools but bullying is
so damaging and has such serious consequences when it rears its ugly head, that it is
worth finding the time to tackle it.

ORGANISATIONAL ISSUES
WITHIN THE SCHOOL

Below we take a look at factors in the school
environment which may affect behaviour.

If there are school environmental factors
which seem to be contributing to bullying and
bad behaviour they need to be tackled.

1. The school playground is the major area for
   bullying behaviour in schools. While it is
   important to have strict, effective supervision, it has been shown that behaviour
   has greatly improved where play facilities
   (games painted on to the playground surface,
   play equipment, such as slides or swings,
   team games organised, benches in quiet
   areas for reading, chatting or playing board
   games, etc.) have been provided. Aggressive
   behaviour, squabbling, mischevious tricks on
   others and bullying have all been reduced
   in these circumstances.

   In addition to the fun which the children
   experience, their social skills have also
   improved and the relationship between
   teachers and pupils, and between the pupils
   themselves, has improved. If pupils are to
   participate in the games social skills, such

as taking your turn, accepting defeat, two-way communication and making decisions, are all involved.

It is advisable that teachers, pupils and playground supervisors (if you have them) be involved in the planning in this area of change. I know from experience that where pupils, with support, information and encouragement from teachers, were involved in this process it definitely worked and incidents of bullying decreased. A further bonus was that after the initial stages, the intensity and stress of supervision on teachers decreased. The children were occupied and there was less rough play and/or bullying during break times, previously a time when bullying was most likely to occur.

2. When pupils are cooped up indoors during bad weather, trouble, and bullying, can occur. Having a supply of board games in classrooms to occupy the pupils during breaks is invaluable. In some schools the practice of teaching pupils how to play chess, draughts and other games has developed with benefits to everyone. Schools have done great work in this area and a very trying and difficult time for pupils and teachers has been transformed into an enjoyable one.

This may, initially, mean more organisation and work for teachers, but the benefits will far outweigh the problems. With direction and guidance, the pupils will take responsibility for distributing, collecting and keeping the games in good repair. The parents can certainly be involved here in coaching the children, if they have experience of the games.

As one teacher in a large suburban school told me:

> *Break-times on wet days used to be a real strain for the teachers but since we introduced board games and allowed our 6th classes to use the table tennis, life is much more pleasant for everyone.*

In this school it was mainly parents who came in to teach the children how to play draughts and chess. They also played snakes and ladders, ludo and Connect 4 with the infants and juniors. A store of drawing paper (plain or with templates for colouring) and some crayons are invaluable for infants and juniors.

3. Other areas such as toilets, wash rooms, sports' rooms and corridors, if they are causing problems, may need to be supervised more carefully or systems put in place to ensure that pupils do not misbehave in them. The ancillary staff may be able to support teachers in these areas of the school.

4. Studies in Britain and in the USA have shown that much bullying takes place on the school bus. Several pupils, with whom I spoken, have told me that they hated travelling on the bus. They found it to be stressful and distressing because of horse-play, objects being thrown, teasing, public ridicule and/or "non-stop slagging".

   This is definitely an area for the whole school community to look at and parents are pivotal in ensuring that their own children behave and do not bully others coming and going to school. It can be extremely difficult, even unsafe, for the driver to have to drive as well as supervise. The driver cannot manouevre a bus and, at the same time, try to maintain discipline.

There has to be a clear understanding of what is expected of everyone, particularly pupils, and a structure in place to ensure this. Each school community has to work out their own procedures.

5. Entering and leaving the school at different times during the day can cause a great amount of shoving and pushing and aggressive behaviour. This can result in a number of pupils suffering daily harrassment which can be prevented if there are procedures to ensure that pupils come and go in an orderly fashion.

6. Care must be taken that stories, teaching materials or equipment dealing with travellers, colour, race or any type of prejudice, which might cause some pupils to be offended or to become objects of ridicule, are not used. Jokes dealing with colour, race, foreigners, disability or mannerisms should never be tolerated.

7. Everything possible should be done to ensure that nicknames are not used within the school community. Nicknames can cause ongoing distress to adults and pupils and their use should not be allowed. Discussions on nicknames should be undertaken, involving staff, parents and, most importantly, pupils.

Even where pupils appear to accept and

tolerate nicknames you will find that there is some damage being done to them as regards their self-worth and their perception of how their peers view them.

It is of benefit to pupils encourage them to call each other by first names and to treat each other respectfully.

Some months ago, I witnessed a discussion among a group of 6th class pupils (28 pupils:16 girls and 12 boys) on nicknames during a 'circle-time' session. The pain and hurt experienced by pupils was openly expressed. I was struck by the accuracy of the nicknames, as they related to mannerisms or particular physical features of individual pupils and the deep hurt which they caused. The great majority of pupils did not want nicknames either in school or outside. They indicated that they would welcome support from teachers on this issue. Adults can be dismissive of nicknames, and I am aware of many situations where even parents have tolerated the use of nicknames for their own children.

THE ACTION: WHAT HAPPENS IF BULLYING OCCURS OR IS SUSPECTED?

Dealing with Incidents of Bullying

Through consultation with pupils and parents a series of procedures can be developed to be followed when bullying, which is clearly defined, takes place. These procedures, in so far as it is possible, can indicate:

✦   what steps are to be taken;

✦   what is to be recorded;

✦   what sanctions if any are to be invoked;

✦   whether or not parents are to be informed;

✦   who else should be informed;

✦   what support if any the bully or victim may need and what support we can offer or access.

Sanctions

✦   A series of fair and appropriate sanctions is needed to reflect the seriousness of a bullying incident.

✦   A ticking off may be adequate for an incident of name-calling or teasing.

✦   A punishment of detention or withdrawl of privileges may be used if there are ongoing attempts to hurt and humiliate.

✦   Involvement of parents should be sought if there is any question of a pupil being a persistent bully or in the event of a serious incident.

The object is not to punish if possible but to get the pupil to understand why the behaviour has to change and then to change it.

    The aim is to:

✦   rehabilitate, not annihilate, the pupil;

✦   work out a code which recognises and affirms good behaviour and endeavours to eradicate bad, anti-social behaviour.

✦   avoid making an example of a pupil as

this is dangerous and ineffective. If pupils, irrespective of what they have done, feel humiliated or feel that they have become an object of ridicule they will be hurt and angry and as a consequence may decide to continue with the bad behaviour. Fear may stop some of them temporarily, but as their attitude will not have changed they will feel hard done by and very likely take up the old behaviour at another time.

Suspected Bullying

If bullying is suspected, all involved should be spoken with and questioned, including the suspected bully(ies), victim(s) and any witnesses.

It is not advisable to question pupils in public or, initially, as a group. Questioning as a group may result in the victim or witnesses being afraid to tell the full story. It is better for everyone if they are questioned individually, and outside the classroom.

In the case of the bully the objective is not to humiliate or on the other hand to allow him/her to entertain the other pupils, which can happen in a public situation.

Even if you cannot get to the bottom of what is happening, word about what you have done will filter through to the other pupils and you will send a strong message to everyone involved that you are on the alert, and ready to take action.

BULLYING IDENTIFIED

If bullying is identified, again all involved should be spoken to and questioned individually. Support and protection should be offered to the victim, and the bully should be disciplined.

We should not hesitate to inform parents if we have any doubts about our ability to resolve the situation satisfactorily. Even if pupils appear to have recovered, the bullying may have gone much deeper than is evident to us and, long after the problem appears to have been sorted out, it can still cause the victim pain as he/she tries to regain self-confidence.

Informing Parents

Parents definitely need to be informed if we suspect that:

✦   the bully may re-offend;

✦   the bully does not understand the gravity of his/her behaviour;

✦   the bully needs ongoing support from parents or professional help;

✦   the victim is still fearful and needs to have his/her confidence supported;

✦   the victim might become involved in a similiar situation again;

✦   the victim needs support and/or professional help.

Help is Available

At all times it must be made clear to the bullies
and the victims that help and support are
available if they choose to seek it. You can
give appropriate assistance to either party if
you think it will help.

Action and Procedures

The degree of discipline which will be admin-
istered to a pupil who bullies will depend on
the gravity and nature of the incident. You
cannot dictate for every incident as contexts
are different.

However, you need a set of agreed procedures in place to deal with the majority of incidents. Punishment is only used as a last resort
and, for instance, in the case of a once-off
incident, it should be minimal.

All pupils and parents will be informed in
writing of the school's attitude to bullying,
positive behaviour and disciplinary procedures
and punishments (see Appendix 3).

Procedures Which have been Used with Some Success

All or some of these will be used depending on
the gravity of the offence.

+   All incidents are recorded on incident
     sheets and filed (see Appendix 2).

+   Offending pupils will be informed that the
     incident is being recorded.

+   Parents will generally be informed: it is
     advisable to inform both sets of parents.

✦ An official, noted warning not to re-offend will be given.

✦ Punishments will range from:

(a) an apology to the victim. Public apologies are not advisable. After a private apology the message will permeate through to the other students;

(b) a written assurance that the incident will not be repeated;

(c) exclusion from a school activity on one or two occasions: a school trip to the swimming pool, a game or some leisure pursuit. You have to be particularly selective in using this 'weapon';

(d) being escorted to and from school by a parent for two/three days or weeks, depending on the gravity of the situation. The pupil will be requested to fill in a behaviour report sheet and have it signed for instance by the class teacher or the teacher who investigated the incident. Pupils find this to be very tiresome and trying;

(e) a written account of the incident and the pupil's plans for the future, written by the pupil;

(f) if two pupils cannot relate civilly to one another it may be better to keep them separated as far as possible in school;

(g) an interview with the bully in the presence of his or her parents.

If there are repeated incidents parents will have to be brought into the process of directly supporting the school in line with the guidelines issued by the Department of Education. (Guidelines on countering bullying behaviour in primary and post-primary schools (1993) Department of Education Government Publications).

As a last resort, the board of management will become directly involved. Suspension may be invoked at this stage.

Get Everyone to Join In

At the end of the day the easiest and most effective way to combat bullying is to get everyone in the school community to join together and to work together for this purpose. The aim has to be to create an atmosphere of non-acceptance of bullying.

When every pupil and adult (teachers, parents and other members of staff) is clear about what the feeling and policy in the school is in relation to bullying, and when they are not afraid or ashamed to do whatever is necessary to stop themselves, or others, being bullied, the school will be a healthy and safe environment for all.

Appendix 1

A bullying awareness week (having a strong curricular base & a high level of parental involvement)

HOW DOES IT WORK ?

A bullying awareness week "can be an enjoyable and fruitful project for all in the school community. It involves a period of time during which there will be a "planned" focus on bullying. Everyone in the school will be involved in some activity related to bullying: parents, pupils, maintenance staff, the bus driver, the traffic warden, the local community, the teachers and the board of management.

A set period of time is allocated where through different types of related class activities and some project work there is almost total focus on the following areas.

+ Raising awareness of bullying, and learning about the detrimental effects it has on our lives.

+ Creating the confidence within the school community which ensures that everyone will protect their own and other's rights, and take action by report bullying, or suspected bullying. You want people with a high sense of self-worth, who do not bully others, and do not allow themselves to be bullied.

✦ Building on and adding to the climate of trust, respect, equality, kindness, care and consideration for others in the school community.

Motto for the Week

A starting point can be to devise a motto for the week. All we need is a simple statement of what we hope to achieve, or the school philosophy. For example:

In St Paul's adults and pupils (or pupils and staff) treat each other with respect. We do not bully, or tolerate bullying.

or

In St Paul's we believe that every member of our school community has equal rights. We all work for each other to ensure that we can learn, play and live together without bullying.

or

Keeping St Paul's a bully-free school begins with me.

or

St Paul's pupils and staff work together to create a peaceful and happy school environment where everyone is safe and happy.

THE ACTIVITIES

1. Pupils work on bullying through:

+ creative writing;

+ art competitions (pictures & posters);

+ group collage of bullying situations, streamers, banners;

+ the work produced should be put on public display;

+ gymnastics;

+ drama and mime;

+ storytelling; their own experiences of bullying or reading stories from literature or literature for their peers;

+ class discussion and debate;

+ classwork on definite planned sections of programmes such as 'The Stay-Safe Programme' or 'On my own two feet'.

Each class has a number of planned periods dealing with sections of these, or other programmes. You ensure that every child deals with the broad aspects of bullying in class during the week. This is a key part of any bullying awareness week/day.

2. Parents and other staff work together and with teaching staff on bullying through:

+ participating in creative writing, or art competitions (this has been done very successfully);

✦   telling their stories of bullying to pupils, telling about incidents from their own school days;

✦   reading from literature to pupils;

✦   attending and supporting the pupils' drama presentations;

✦   attending talks (very often information evenings or mornings, followed by discussion, which are facilitated by parents/teachers/psychologists, on bullying, or related topics, These talks are organised by the Parents' Association, or the board of management, and can provide information on the different issues related to bullying, raise awareness of bullying, and examine the attitudes of teachers, parents and other adults towards bullying;

✦   working with teachers on organising competitions for pupils or the wider community;

✦   obtaining sponsorship;

✦   organising displays;

✦   informing the wider community of the school's efforts (ethos)and involving them;

✦   Seminars/discussion groups/videos on topics relating to bullying, for parents, pupils, teachers and the wider community.

It is important to examine the School Code on preventing and countering bullying during the week.

Raising awareness, examining attitudes and providing information for parents, teachers and other staff, will be the main focus of the work done here.

3. Teachers work on bullying through:

+ organising creative classwork or projects on bullying;

+ organising drama from the class or an outside drama group;

+ accessing literature for pupils on bullying;

+ relating stories of their own;

+ organising competitions;

+ working with parents on displays and parents' inputs;

+ organising sponsorship for the competitions.

4. The wider community

As the school is very much part of the wider community it is important to involve them in events such as the bullying awareness week. They can further develop confidence in the school from attending activities during the week (e.g. the writing or art displays or the drama), and/or provide sponsorship for some of the events.

AFTER OUR BULLYING AWARENESS EXERCISE

Subsequent to the "week" the school can produce a magazine outlining the events of the week. In addition to being a celebration of all of the school's activity the magazine can be used by parents or teachers later on to reinforce the anti-bullying message. A copy of the school's code on bullying can be included.

Teachers, parents and pupils, who are involved in this awareness raising exercise, will learn a lot of new things about bullying, how it affects people, and the need for agreed action when incidents take place

WILL OUR SCHOOL BE SEEN AS HAVING A PROBLEM?

Some teachers and parents had fears that having a bullying awareness week might send out a message that their school had a problem with bullying, but thankfully this has not been the case in any school where I know that the exercise has been undertaken. In fact, the focus on bullying for a week enhanced the pupils', teachers', parents' and the wider community's confidence in the school. The school sent out a strong message that they would leave no stone unturned to keep bullying out of the school.

Appendix 2

Examples of bullying incident sheets

A BULLYING INCIDENT SHEET FOR THE TEACHER

Name of pupil: _____

Class/year: _____

Teacher/form tutor: _____

Details of incident

Date: _____

Where it occurred: _____

Who was involved: _____

What happened: _____

Who was informed (please tick)

Parents: _____

Class/Form teacher: _____

Principal: _____

Other: _____

Follow up:

Any other relevant information:

_____

_____

Signed: _____

Date: _____

When you have filled this form in, it is useful and beneficial to read it out to the pupil(s) involved. This document may be requested by a parent.

A BULLYING INCIDENT SHEET
FOR THE PUPIL
(TO BE FILLED OUT IN PRIVATE)

Name of pupil: _____

Class/year: _____

Teacher/Form tutor: _____

Details of incident

Date: _____

Where it occurred: _____

Who was involved: _____

What happened: a full description:

_____
_____
_____
_____
_____
_____
_____
_____

Do you know the school's code on bullying:

_____

What do you intend to do now?

_____

_____

_____

Any other comments:

_____

_____

_____

Signed: _____

Date: _____

The teacher may also decide to sign this form. A copy of the form should be kept in the school.

The student should be requested to read out what he/she has written to you and/or the parents, principal or another teacher who is involved (not to the class) and questions may be asked to clarify issues.

Other pupil's accounts may be read out to the group involved in the incident to cross check.

Remember pupils never deserve public humiliation.

Appendix 3

Information sheets on bullying

SAMPLES OF INFORMATION SHEETS TO BE GIVEN TO PARENTS AND PUPILS

1. For Parents

St Paul's School
Dublin 6.

Parents keep our school bully free

Dear parents

St Paul's is a caring school where we all work together. Bullies are not welcome in our school and we all work together to stop bullying. Every pupil and adult in St Paul's is valuable and valued and must be treated with respect.

We will do everything possible to prevent bullying, but we need your co-operation. We know that bullying of any type can affect your child's health, ability to learn, happiness and overall development.

If we all work together we will succeed.

Remember that children who are bullied often become very angry and resentful and "children simmering with resentment are not in the right frame of mind for learning".

Thank you.
The Staff of St Paul's

What to tell your child if he/she is being bullied:

1. You must tell someone if you are being bullied or if you know that someone else is being bullied. Bullies will be dealt with promptly and immediately in St Paul's.

2. Tell someone - a teacher, the principal, your parents or an adult you can trust. Remember, if you cannot protect yourself you must seek help.

3. Parents are asked to tell the school authorities if for some reason a pupil is afraid to do so.

4. If you are being bullied and you are on your own scream, shout, run towards an adult or a house where you see signs of activity.

5. Do not stop looking for help until the bullying stops.

6. If you keep bullying a secret we, the parents or the school authorities, will not be able to help you.

7. Do not strike back at a bully, tell someone.

Remember you are equal to every other pupil in the school. If you do not tell someone the bully will see you as weak. The bully loves your silence.

2. Information Sheet on Bullying for Pupils in St Paul's School

Dear pupils

St Paul's is a caring school where we all work together. Bullies are not welcome in our school and we all work together to stop bullying. Every pupil and adult in St Paul's is valuable and valued and must be treated with respect.

You help a bully continue when you do not tell someone who can stop the bullying. None of us deserve to suffer at the hands of a bully. Remember if you are being bullied it is not your fault. Bullies enjoy making you feel small, hurting you or damaging your property. You cannot learn, play or feel well if we are being bullied.

Mabye you should ask yourself the question:

"Would the bully act like this if my teacher or parent was here?"

If he or she would not, then you can be sure that you are being bullied.

Thank you.
The Staff of St Paul's

What to do if you are being bullied:

1. Tell someone. It is good for you and everyone else if you do.

2. Tell your parents, a teacher or an adult who can help.

3. Do not stop telling (or yelling!!) until you get help. Remember, nobody has the right to make you unhappy or hurt you.

4.   If you are on your own scream, shout, yell, do whatever you have to or run to somewhere safe.

5.   Bullies enjoy causing pain, and if you do not tell someone they will continue to bully you and others.

Remember you are equal to every other pupil in the school. If you do not tell someone the bully will see you as weak. The bully loves your silence.

Appendix 4

Samples of questionnaires

You can pick and choose questions from these lists to meet you own requirements. About 10 to 12 questions will be enough. It is worthwhile giving these type of questionnaires to find out among other things:

+ What are the attitudes towards bullying?

+ Who is being bullied in the school?

+ What type of bullying takes place?

+ Who are the bullies?

+ What do people think bullying is?

+ How do pupils think bullying is dealt with in the school?

Sample 1

QUESTIONNAIRE FOR PUPILS

Please answer these questions honestly. We want to make sure that we do not have bullying in our school and what you tell us is important. You need not write your name on the page, just write in the words in (a), (b) and (c) that tell us what we want to know.

(a) I am a _____ (male/female).

(b) I am in _____ class.

(c) I am _____ years old.

(Check before the pupils start that these questions are filled in properly.)

1. In what ways can you be bullied?

2. What do you think is the worst type of bullying?

3. Have you ever been bullied in school?

4. If yes, describe what happened?

5. How did you feel?

6. Did you tell anyone about it?

7. If yes, who did you tell?

8. What action was taken?

9. Were you happy with the action?

10. If you did not tell anyone, why did you decide not to tell?

11. Have you been bullied in the last two weeks?

12. What happened?

13. Why do you think that you were bullied?

14. Why do you think that some pupils bully?

15. Why do you think that some pupils are bullied rather than others?

16. Can we sometimes ignore bullying?

17. What makes you feel safe in school?

18. Could you feel safer in school if something else was done?

19. Have you seen bullying in the last month?

20. Did you do anything to stop it?

21. If yes, what did you do?

22. If you did not, why not?

23. Is the school the type of school where you feel comfortable in reporting bullying?

24. Do you think that enough is done when you report it?

25. What more do you think could be done?

26. If you were being bullied who would you tell?

Thank you for completing this questionnaire.

Sample 2

QUESTIONNAIRE FOR PARENTS

Please answer these questions honestly. We want to make sure that we do not have bullying in our school and what you tell us is important. You need not write your name on the page, just write in the words in (a), (b) and (c) that tell us what we want to know.

(a)   I am a _____ (male or female).

(b)   I am _____ years old.

(c)   I have _____ sons and _____ daughters in this school.

(d)   Which classes are they in. (e.g. infants, 1st, 2nd, 3rd, 4th, etc.)

   Boys   Girls

   _____   _____

   _____   _____

1.   In what ways do you think children can be bullied?

2.   Why do you think that some pupils are bullies?

3.   Why do you think that some pupils are bullied rather than others?

4.   Have your children ever been bullied?

5.   Why do you think that they were bullied?

6.   What did you do about it and what was the result of your action?

7.   Can we sometimes ignore bullying?

8.   Have you observed any bullying during the past two weeks?

9.   Where did it happen?

10. What happened?

11. Did you do anything to stop it?

12. If yes, what did you do?

13. If you did not, why not?

14. Has your child been involved in any bullying?

15. What did you do about?

16. What do you advise your child to do if he/she is being bullied?

17. Is the school the type of school where you can report bullying?

18. Where does most bullying take place in the school?

19. Is enough being done to stop it in the school?

20. What more do you think could be done?

21. If we were all to do one thing in our school to reduce bullying, what do you think that should be?

Thank you for filling in this questionnaire.

Sample 3

QUESTIONNAIRE FOR TEACHERS

Please answer these questions honestly. We want to make sure that we do not have bullying in our school and what you tell us is important. You need not write your name on the page, just write in the words in (a), (b) and (c) that tell us what we want to know.

(a) I am _____ (male or female).

(b) I teach _____ (infants, juniors, middle or seniors).

(c) I teach _____ boys and _____ girls.

(d) I am _____ (a parent or not a parent).

1. What are the most common types of bullying you have to deal with?

2. Where in the school (the trouble spots) does most bullying take place?

3. Have the trouble spots been discussed and attempts made to improve them?

4. What types of children are likely to get involved in bullying others?

    4a. Why is this?

5. Why do you think that some pupils are bullied rather than others?

    5a. How can they be helped?

6. How does bullying affect your pupils?

7. What do you think bullying does to the bully?

8. How do you feel about bullies?

9. Should bullies be helped?

10. Have you seen bullying or had it reported to you during the past two weeks?

11. If yes, please describe what happened?

12. What action was taken?

13. Were you happy with the outcome?

14. Do you include inputs on bullying in your teaching of the curriculum?

15. How do you raise awareness of bullying with your pupils in class?

15a. Have you ideas which you would like to share with your colleagues?

15b. How could this best be done?

16. Have you used any specific programme to deal with bullying, e.g. The Stay-Safe Programme?

17. Have you as a teaching staff discussed bullying?

18. Would you welcome more information for teachers, parents and pupils on bullying?

19. How could this best be done?

20. Are school procedures satisfactory for dealing with bullies, bullying and victims?

21. What do you think could be done to make them even better?

22. What makes it difficult for you to deal with some bullying situations?

23. If we were to do one thing in our school to reduce bullying, what do you think that should be?

Thank you for filling in the questionnaire.

Sample 4

QUESTIONNAIRE FOR ANCILLARY STAFF IN THE SCHOOL

Please answer these questions honestly. We want to make sure that we do not have bullying in our school and what you tell us is important. You need not write your name on the page, just write in the words in (a) and (b) that tell us what we want to know.

(a) I am _____ (a man or woman).
(b) I am _____ (a parent or not a parent).

We thank you as a valuable member of the school team for filling in this questionnaire. Your information, views and opinions will be helpful in putting in place a policy to wipe out bullying in our school.

1. What kinds of bullying have you seen in the school?

2. What kind of bullying do you think happens most often?

3. Could you describe the last bullying incident you saw and when it happened?

4. Did you report it to anyone?

5. If yes, to whom?

6. If no, why did you decide not to report it?

7. Where do you think that most of the bullying takes place in the school?

8. Are there some children who seem to be frequently bullied?

9. Why do you think that they are being bullied?

10. Has any child ever told you about being bullied?

11. What did you advise them to do?

12. Were you happy with your decision?

13. What else would you like to have done in that situation?

14. Would you like to have a talk with some of the teachers about what to do if bullying arises?

15. What do you think could be done about bullying in the school that is not already being done?

16. How do you think that you could help in stopping bullying as part of the school team?

Thank you for filling in this questionnaire

Sample 5

A QUESTIONNAIRE FOR
TEACHERS OR PARENTS

Bullying in School
Why do Children Bully?

If you suspect that a pupil/pupils are engaged in bullying you must first of all try to work out the reasons for the behaviour and these will point you towards resolving the problem.

The reasons for pupils bullying can come from a variety of areas.

Read this questionnaire and rank in order of importance (from 1 to 10) the reasons for pupils bullying others.

List from 1 to 10 *in order of importance* what you think are the reasons why children bully.

1.   They are jealous of other pupils.

     _____

2.   They want to get attention, and show off for others.

     _____

3.   They are told to do it by other bullies and they bully so as not to be left out and to prove themselves.

     _____

4. For some reason they enjoy humuliating, hurting and making others miserable.

    _____

5. They are being bullied by others and want some revenge.

    _____

6. They have not a sense of being fair and they are bad losers.

    _____

7. Bossing others and shoving them around makes them feel good.

    _____

8. They are not used to taking turns and sharing and they always want their own way.

    _____

9. They are disturbed and need help from doctors or others.

    _____

10. They feel bad about themselves and they take it out on others.

    _____

11. They find it difficult to make friends, or to keep friends.

    _____

12. There is a lot of bullying in their home.

    _____

13. They cannot feel or see other pupil's pain when they hurt them.

    _____

14. They believe that strong people should dominate and bully weaker people.

    _____

15. They feel picked on at school and they are are angry.

    _____

16. They enjoy bullying and they know that they will get away with it.

    _____

17. They have not been told, or if the have they do not clearly understand, that bullying is not acceptable in the school.

    _____

19. Bullying is their way of frightening others and showing their power.

    _____

20. They cannot enjoy other pupils successes in class or at games.

    _____

Thank you for filling in this questionnaire

Sample 6

A QUESTIONNAIRE ON BULLYING IN GENERAL

Please read these statements about bullying and think about them. Then rank ten of them in order of importance.

Place the numbers 1 to 10 beside the ones you choose as most important in terms of bullying as you see it.

We can talk about some of these statements later if you wish.

1.   We can bully others through our actions, words and gestures.

      _____

2.   A bully takes pleasure out of hurting others and humiliating them.

      _____

3.   Bullies are clever, and do most of their work in secret.

      _____

4.   Teachers should never criticise a bully in public. He/she will only become worse.

      _____

5.   Bullies only think of themselves.

      _____

6. Bullies always feel bad about themselves.

  _____

7. If we beat or strike people who bully others, they may think that their own behaviour was correct.

  _____

8. Too much bullying behaviour goes unchecked in society.

  _____

9. Aggressive parents are responsible for aggressive children.

  _____

10. A bully can be a bully because of his/her experiences in life.

  _____

11. Bullies are always to blame for their behaviour.

  _____

12. Victims must never feel guilty because they have been bullied.

  _____

13. Only strong people bully.

  _____

14. Bullying can create major problems for people.

  _____

15. Bullying affects your ability to learn.

  _____

16. If you are strong you should help those who are weak.

_____

17. If you are being bullied you should tell someone or you are helping a bully.

_____

18. Bullies often need help and advice themselves.

_____

19. Bullies choose who to pick on.

_____

20. All bullies are unpopular and have few friends.

_____

21. It is not a sign of weakness to ask for help.

_____

22. Bullying sometimes is allowed to continue because we do not tell the people who should be told.

_____

23. Every kind of bullying is equally bad.

_____

24. Sometimes we have to avoid bullies.

_____

25. Bullying is undeserved by victims and they have a right to seek help.

_____

26. Name-calling is really not bullying.

_____

27. We should help others if they are being bullied.

_____

28. Bullies love us to keep bullying a secret.

_____

29. Bullies make people do things for them through fear.

_____

30. People of every age can bully or be bullied.

_____

Thank you for filling in this questionnaire

Sample 7

AN AWARENESS-RAISING
QUESTIONNAIRE

Bullying in School

An exercise in raising awareness of, and finding out about, bullying.

There are 21 questions/statements here. You will probably decide not to use them all, depending on what is happening in your school and the class you are dealing with.

The questionnaire could be given to teachers and parents.

Please read the statements listed below and write in *true* or *false* after each.

1.   Some people, who are annoying, deserve to be bullied.

    _____

2.   Only children bully others.

    _____

3.   Boys bully as much as girls.

    _____

4.   Bullying toughens you up and helps you deal with life.

    _____

5.   When you isolate someone and get others to join you in doing it you are bullying.

_____

6.   The best way to treat a bully is to give the bully a taste of his or her own medicine.

_____

7.   Parents who bully give bad messages to their children.

_____

8.   When we are picked on, we isolate ourselves and feel bad about ourselves.

_____

9.   Most bullying in school takes place in the playground.

_____

10.   There is a difference between rough play and bullying.

_____

11.   Bullying is part of growing up. It is good for you.

_____

12.   All bullies are big and strong and rough.

_____

13.   Nobody deserves to be bullied or should allow themselves to be bullied.

_____

14.   There is always someone to tell if we are being bullied.

_____

15. You are weak and ought to be ashamed if you have to go and ask for help if you are being bullied.

   _____

16. It is good to talk to someone and ask for help if we need it.

   _____

17. We must not allow bullying or bullies to hide in our school.

   _____

18. Every pupil in a school has a right to be happy and to be allowed to learn.

   _____

19. Some children are bullied because others are jealous of them.

   _____

20. Bullies are not popular in their class or school.

   _____

21. Bullies cannot think of others because they are so wrapped up in themselves.

   _____

Thank you for filling in this questionnaire

GENERAL POINTS RELATING
TO THE QUESTIONNAIRES

When we are asking for *true* or *false* answers, most of the questions or statements are not so clear-cut.

After they have filled out the questionnaire ask individual children to comment on any of the questions/statements and start a discussion about any of the issues around them. You must be prepared to deal with issues and situations which may arise during the class discussion.

Most pupils find the questionnaires interesting and enjoy the exercise. However, some pupils who are involved in bullying and who feel uncomfortable with the exercise may try to ridicule what is being done and in a sense through their dismissive, even jeering approach try to bully others into non-participation. This is a situation to watch out for.

There may be some ambivalent attitudes among the pupils around bullying (everyone is bullied at sometime and you have to put up with it; my Dad said that he was bullied and it never did him any harm), which you may gently tease out.

Many issues can arise and much useful information can be elicited. These will give direction for strategies which can be used in tackling bullying and ensuring that everyone in the school community works to protect the pupils from being preyed on by bullies.

The questionnaires should be given to representatives of each group throughout the school. The number of people chosen to fill them in, will depend on the size of the school. The completed questionnaires can be corrected by a small group chosen by you for the purpose. Your school will have to make its own decisions in this area.

The information which will be obtained will form the basis for laying out your policy and point you in the direction in which you need to work. You will know where you are at and where you want to go from here.

Irrespective of the level of bullying, or even if is not part of what is happening in the school at present, every year a new cohort of pupils will enter the school and some of them will be vulnerable to bullying themselves or being bullied. You have to be on the alert at all times because of the seriousness of the nature of bullying when it arises. Check out what is happening.

Appendix 5

An outline of a school's response to bullying

As effective, caring school communities, our response to bullying has to be quite definite and clear. Bullying is totally unacceptable and there must be no ambivalence or equivocation and no acceptance of some of the dangerous myths which prevail about bullying.

✦ Bullying is not normal behaviour and damages growth and development of the bully and the victim.

✦ No child, irrespective of how they behave or are perceived to behave, deserves to be bullied.

✦ Bullying is behaviour which is aggressive or which is meant to hurt and will not be tolerated.

✦ We have clear, positive, agreed guidelines for pupils and teachers to follow.

✦ If you have been involved in bullying as an individual or in a group situation and you give a definite commitment not to be involved again that is fine.

✦ We promote helpful behaviour and we take action against bullies.

✦ The safety and happiness of pupils is given priority to ensure that we can live together and support one another.

✦   It is important that pupils let adults in the school community know about bullying situations.

✦   It is recognised that adults in the community must work to create the environment that encourages pupils to talk when they are bullied.

✦   Our school expects that parents, teachers and pupils will work together to prevent, or counter, bullying.

✦   We have a policy on countering bullying and we review it regularly to check how effective it is.

Appendix 6
Organisational issues within schools

Look at factors in the school environment which may affect behaviour. If there are school environmental factors which it is deemed are contributing to bullying and bad behaviour they need to be tackled.

1. The school playground is the major area for bullying behaviour in schools. While it is important to have strict, effective supervision, it has been shown that behaviour has greatly improved where play facilities (games painted on to the playground surface, play equipment, such as slides or swings, team games are organised, benches in quiet areas for reading, chatting or playing board games) have been provided aggressive behaviour, squabbling, mischevious tricks on others and bullying have been reduced.

    In addition to the fun which the children experience, their social and motor skills are improved and the relationship between teachers and pupils, and between the pupils themselves is improved. If pupils are to participate in the games, social skills, such as taking your turn, accepting defeat, two-way communication and making decisions, are all involved.

It is advisable that teachers, pupils and playground supervisors (if you have them) are involved in the planning in this area of change. I know from experience that where pupils, with support, inform-ation and encouragement from teachers, were involved in this process it definitely worked and incidents of bullying decreas-ed. A further bonus was that after the initial stages, the intensity and stress of supervision on teachers decreased. The children were occupied and there was less rough play and/or bullying during break-times, which was when bullying was most likely to happen.

2.   When pupils are cooped up indoors during bad weather, trouble and even bullying can occur. Having a supply of board games in classrooms to occupy the pupils during breaks is invaluable. In some schools the practice of teaching pupils how to play chess, draughts and other games has developed with benefits to everyone. Schools have done great work in this area and a very trying and difficult time for pupils and teachers has been transformed into an enjoyable one.

This may initially mean more organ-isation and work for teachers, but the benefits will make it well worth it. With direction and guidance the pupils will take responsibility for distributing, coll-ecting and keeping the games in good repair. Parents can certainly be involved here in coaching the children if they have experience of the games.

As one teacher in a large suburban school told me:

Break-times on wet days used to be a real strain for the teachers, but since we introduced board games and allowed our 6th classes to play table tennis in the sports hall, life is much more pleasant for everyone.

In this instance, it was mainly parents who came in to teach the children how to play draughts and chess. They also played snakes and ladders, ludo and Connect 4 with the infants and juniors. A store of drawing paper (plain or with templates for colouring) and some crayons are invaluable for infants and juniors.

3. Other areas, such as toilets, wash rooms, sports' rooms and corridors, if they are causing problems, may need to be supervised more carefully or systems put in place to ensure that pupils do not misbehave in them. The ancillary staff may be able to support teachers in these areas of the school.

4. Studies in Britain and in the USA have shown that much bullying takes place on the school bus. Several pupils, with whom I have spoken, told me that they hated travelling on the bus. They found it to be stressful and distressing because of horseplay, objects being thrown, teasing, public ridicul and/or "non-stop slagging".

This is definitely an area for the whole school community to look at and parents are pivotal in ensuring that their own children behave and do not bully others coming and going to school. It can be extemely difficult, even unsafe, for the driver to have to drive as well as supervise. The driver cannot manouevre a bus and at the same time try to maintain discipline.

There has to be a clear understanding of what is expected of everyone, particularly pupils, and a structure in place to ensure this. Each school community has to work out its own procedures.

5. There can be a great deal of shoving and pushing and aggressive behaviour when pupils are entering or leaving the school. This can result in a number of pupils suffering daily harrassment which can be prevented if there are procedures to ensure that pupils come and go in an orderly fashion.

6. Care must be taken that stories, teaching materials or equipment dealing with travellers, colour, race or any type of prejudice, which might cause some pupils to be offended or to become objects of ridicule, are not used. Jokes dealing with colour, race, foreigners, disability or mannerisms should never be tolerated.

7. Everything possible should be done to ensure that nicknames are not used within the school community. Nicknames can cause ongoing distress to adults and pupils and their use should not be allowed. Discussions on nicknames can be undertaken by staff, parents and, most importantly, pupils.

Even where pupils appear to accept and tolerate nicknames you will find that there is some damage being done to them as regards their self-worth and how their peers view them. It is of benefit to pupils to encourage them to call each other by first names and to treat each other respectfully.

Some months ago, I witnessed a discussion among a group of 6th class pupils (28 pupils: 16 girls and 12 boys) on nicknames during a 'circle time' session. The pain and hurt experienced by pupils was openly expressed. I was struck by the accuracy of the nicknames as they related to mannerisms or particular physical features of individual pupils and the deep hurt which they caused. The great majority of pupils did not want nicknames either in school or outside. The children indicated that they would welcome support from teachers on this issue. Adults can be dismissive of nicknames, and I am aware of many situations where parents have even allowed their children to have nicknames labelled on to them.

Appendix 7

A child is being bullied: what are the signs?

In most cases, if there is a child being bullied in school, in the home or somewhere outside the home, the intervention of the teachers and parents can stop the bullying. You can find situations:

+ where older brothers or sisters are defending younger siblings over-zealously;

+ involving an ongoing row where one child blames another for getting them into trouble;

+ of pure and simple dislike of one child by another;

+ where a child becomes the butt of bullying behaviour, cruel teasing or jokes of a gang or class;

+ where a mistaken view of what a joke is which has caused a child to be regularly made feel bad.

These situations in themselves, if not checked, can be very serious but once tackled firmly, fairly and decisively, they generally be stopped.

However, other situations can be more problematic and can occur at any age from 2 to 18. Recognising and pinpointing the bullying problem can be difficult because your child has not told you about it and, even though you strongly suspect it is happening, he/she strongly denies it when questioned.

BULLIES CAN FRIGHTEN
VICTIMS INTO SILENCE

It is important to remember that bullies work by using fear and intimidation and get what they want through frightening others. They do not want their actions to be known by adults who might be in a position to take action against them. So they often threaten their victims with injury to themselves, their property, their relatives if they 'rat' on them. A bully can exert extraordinary power over a victim into remaining silent.

Remember that bullies do not abide by the normal rules for behaving. They can be clever and vicious in frightening others into:

✦   not telling or seeking support from adults;

✦   becoming passive to please them;

✦   thinking that they have to accept what is being doled out, to be resigned to their fate or worse treatment awaits them;

✦   feeling that, irrespective of what they do, the bully will be able to get back at them;

✦   feeling that they are deserving of being bullied. The bully makes them believe that something about themselves, their families or something they are doing causes them to be bullied. They make the victim feel guilty and feel bad about himself or herself.

It is important to remember that, irrespective of how open and close the communication is between you and your child, if he/she is being bullied he/she may be too frightened to tell you. The terror which the bully has instilled into his/her mind will prevent disclosure being made by your child to you.

SOME POSSIBLE SIGNS TO WATCH OUT FOR

If your child is being bullied it can manifest itself in many ways, through a change in behaviour, a change in play habits, moodiness, a general demeanour and appearance of un-happiness, outburts of anger or even through almost total withdrawl into himself or herself. If they are being hurt and subjected to pain and humiliation outside the home, and are unable to do anything about it, they may react negatively, either aggressively or over pass-ively, towards the family and take out their frustrations in the home.

You may suspect that bullying is to blame for your child's behaviour but you are unable to put a finger on what is happening. You have not observed anything that should cause your child's fear, anxiety or worry. You may have noticed that your child's behaviour and moods have changed over a short period of time and he/she, though visibly anxious or upset, insists that everything is fine. This change in your child may be exemplified by:

+   unhappiness in school and a reluctan-ance to get up in the mornings;

+   wanting to be collected in the evenings and appearing to be very apprehensive leaving school;

+   often complaining about feeling sick in the mornings without any visible physical signs;

+   a deterioration in work accompanied by a lessening in interest in school and work;

+ being liable to become upset or cry for the smallest reason;

+ being reluctant to go out and play as was usual;

+ being unusually negative about issues;

+ making comments and statements that downgrade himself/herself;

+ appearing to be generally unhappy;

+ being late home from school without any plausible reasons;

+ cuts and/or bruises on the body where the explanations are not really credible;

+ school books, sports' gear or toys go missing regularly and can't be accounted for;

+ developing a sudden interest in self-defence magazines or activities and wanting to join a club. When you talk about this you may get hints as to what is happening, whether it is a leisure interest or a means of striking back. This happens particularly during the 15-18 age range.

+ becoming uneasy or uneccessarily upset when particular peers at school are mentioned.

+ you find that your child is not his or her normal herself and you are asking yourself why is this happening, trying to put the pieces together and trying to get to the bottom of what is going on.

Having looked at what is happening you may decide that your child is being bullied and it is time to take action.

Appendix 8

Recommended Reference Material

V E Besag, *Bullies and Victims in Schools: A Guide to Understanding and Management* (UK: OPU) 1989.

B Byrne, *Bullying: A Community Approach* (Dublin: Columba Press) 1994.

B Byrne, *Coping with Bullying in Schools* (Dublin: Columba Press) 1993. (This is an excellent book.)

INTO, *Enhancing Self-esteem* (Dublin: INTO Publications) 1995.

INTO, *Discipline in the Primary School* (Dublin: INTO Publications) 1993.

G Moss (ed.), *The Basics of Special Needs* (London: Routledge) 1995.

V O'Donnell & CAB O'Donnell, *Bullying: A Resource Guide for Teachers and Parents* (Dublin: Attic Press) 1995.

D Olweus, *Bullying at School: What we know and what we can do* (Oxford: Blackwell Press) 1993.

R Pianta & D Walsh, *High-risk Children in Schools* (London/New York: Routledge) 1996.

K Rigby, *Bullying in Schools and what to do about it* (London: Kingsley) 1997.

E Roland & E Munthe, *Bullying: An International Perspective* (London: Fulton) 1989.

S Skynner & J Cleese, *Families and how to Survive them* (UK: Cedar) 1983.

P Smith & S Sharp (eds), *School Bullying: Insights and Perspectives* (London/New York: Routledge) 1995.

G Stenhouse, *Developing your Child's Self-esteem* (Oxford: Oxford University Press) 1994.

D P Tattum, *Understanding and Managing Bullying* (London: Heinemann) 1993.

D P Tatum & H Lane, *Bullying in Schools* (UK: Trentham Books) 1989.

A Train, *The Bullying Problem* (UK: Souvenir Press) 1995. (This is an excellent book.)

S B Turkel & S Eth, "Psycho-pathological Response to Stress" in Arnold, *Childhood Stress* (New York: Wiley) 1990.